Rama Chandra Ghosha

A Peep into the Vaidik Age

A Brief Survey of Ancient Sanskrit Literature

Rama Chandra Ghosha

A Peep into the Vaidik Age
A Brief Survey of Ancient Sanskrit Literature

ISBN/EAN: 9783742834065

Manufactured in Europe, USA, Canada, Australia, Japa

Cover: Foto ©Andreas Hilbeck / pixelio.de

Manufactured and distributed by brebook publishing software (www.brebook.com)

Rama Chandra Ghosha

A Peep into the Vaidik Age

"A people that can feel no pride in the past, in its history and literature, loses the mainstay of its national character. When Germany was in the very depth of its political degradation, it turned to its ancient literature, and drew hope for the future from the study of the past. Something of the same kind is now passing in India."—*Max Müller.*

A PEEP INTO THE VAIDIK AGE;

OR

A BRIEF SURVEY OF ANCIENT SANSKRIT LITERATURE,

SO FAR AS IT ILLUSTRATES THE DAWN OF ARYAN CIVILIZATION IN INDIA.

BY

RAMACHANDRA GHOSHA.

"THE VEDA HAS A TWO-FOLD INTEREST. IT BELONGS TO THE HISTORY OF THE WORLD AND TO THE HISTORY OF INDIA."—MAX MULLER.

GHOSHA AND BROTHER,—PUBLISHERS.
HIGGINBOTHAM & CO.,—MADRAS.

1879.

To
The revered Memory
OF MY MOTHER,
I INSCRIBE THE FOLLOWING PAGES
WITH ALL THE AFFECTION OF A SON.

PREFACE.

The object of the present volume is to offer to the reader, in a compact form, an outline of the Vedas, or more properly of the ancient Sanskrit Literature, so far as it illustrates the dawn of Aryan civilization in India, which modern investigations have made known to us. The work makes no pretensions to be considered as a complete treatise on the subject; but is intended merely to serve as an introduction to the larger and more systematic works in the English and other European languages; and more especially to help the student in the perusal of original works.

In taking up so extensive and complicated a subject I had to work up the materials which I had collected for many years; and these materials often so much embarrassed me by their copiousness and diversity that I was afraid to benefit from them. There is, indeed, a dense mist of prejudice and preconceived opinions which always impede investigations. But it should be frankly stated that great advances have since been made in the field of Sanskrit research, though much remains as uncertain and unsettled as before. The laborers in the field have now greatly increased; and their researches reflect lasting honor upon them. I shall not give their names here; but I must acknowledge with deep gratitude that I have availed myself of their writings.

It now remains only to be said that I had not the remotest idea to digest and publish the results of researches on the subject owing chiefly to my want of scholarship and to my deficient knowledge of English; but I have ventured upon the task only at the suggestion of Dr. Muir, of Edinburgh, for whom I have the highest respect for his varied learning and Christian piety; and to whom I am highly indebted for the various favors which I have received from him from time to time.

The Vedas are the gigantic labors of the Hindu mind. They have already attracted the attention of some of the best scholars of the far off continents of Europe and America. They are guide-books in all researches into the civilization of the ancient Hindus, on which history can not throw the least light; though it must be admitted that the information to be gleaned from them is but very scanty. Indeed, India never produced a Xenophon or a Thucydides; but nevertheless history can be built up from the materials which lie buried in those ancient documents, simply distinguishing facts from the shoals of mystical legends and mythological drapery which are found to envelop them. The age in which the Vedas and their appendages were composed, has exercised the blandest influence upon all succeeding periods of Indian history; every later branch of literature is closely connected with the Veddik traditions; the religious and moral ideas have been derived from them; the later mythology has also developed out of them; and the Hindu life, in all its aspects, has been moulded by old traditionary precepts.

Though the researches of occidental savans into the Vedas are alike profound and accurate, they carry us into a labyrinth of heterogeneous materials, which to digest and at last present in a readable shape is indeed a hard task. The general deductions and opinions of one Sanskritist in the West are in some cases not found to tally with those of his brother Sanskritist. Thus in many cases they, far from helping us to attain the truth, often throw great doubts and confusion on many an important and salient point. I have, therefore, generally avoided raising issues with them whenever I happened to find myself to differ widely from any one of them on such controverted points, and have only tried to arrive at a definite conclusion whenever that was possible. To claim to have certainly arrived at a literary truth is highly presumptuous in a country such as we live in, where the spirit of Niebuhr has not as yet been attained.

At all events their contributions towards ancient Sanskrit Literature have elucidated many knotty problems; which could never have been solved by the Indian Pandits, who hardly possess a scientific turn of mind; and have at last brought to our knowledge an immense store of information of vital importance which had been so long hid from us by the dishonorable attempts of the Brahmans, who debarred all but themselves from reading the Vedas. It is, however, a curious commentary on the vicissitudes of human affairs that the proud descendants of the holy *Rishis* should consume their midnight oil on the banks of the Ganges, over their sacred books, published for the first time on the banks of the Neckar and the Thames, by those, whom they look upon as *Mlechhas*.

B.

82, JHAMAPUKAR, CALCUTTA:
July, 1879.

ERRATA ET CORRIGENDA.

Page 8, line 4 from foot, for *rifacemento* read *rifacimento*.
Page 9, line 4 from the bottom, for worship read worships.
Page 14, line 3, for Uha-gâna read U'ha-gâna.
,, 14, ,, 5, for Uhyи-gâna read U'hya-gâna.
,, 19, ,, 1, after the White Yajus insert by.
,, 34, ,, 6, for year read years.
,, 34, ,, 11, for 1400-2000 D. C. read 1400-2000.
,, 35, ,, 2 from foot, for as necessary corollary read as a necessary corollary.
,, 38, ,, 2, for reminiscence read reminiscences.
,, 43, ,, 7, for *panchabhuvah* read *pancha-bhuvah*.
,, 47, ,, 10, for *severnan* read *sevenans*.
,, 47, ,, 15, for Bhuiya read Bhujya.
,, 99, ,, 1 from the bottom, for Ritvik read Ritvij.
,, 90, ,, 2 from foot, the same correction.
,, 100, lines 2, 3, the same correction.
,, 107, line 4 from bottom, for the Vâjasaneyi Sanhitâ read the Vâjasaneyi Sanhitâ.
,, 119, ,, 6 from foot, for Century read century.
,, 124, ,, 10, for Atharvamrahasya read Atharvanrahasya.
,, 126, ,, 9, for gotras read gotra.
,, 126 lines 10, 11, 21, 23, 24, the same correction.
,, 139 line 10, for *Akbar* read *Asham*.
,, 149 ,, 3 from the bottom, for Sâkatâyana read Sâkatâyana.
,, 175, ,, 3 from foot, for autchthonous read autochthonous.
,, 179, ,, 13, before From him insert 5.
,, 180 ,, 15 for *menus* read *manus*.

CONTENTS.

PAGES.

vii — ix PREFACE.
1—34 CHAPTER I.
1—28 General Character of the Vedas.
28 The Vaidik Dialect.
28—34 The Chronology of the Vaidik Age.
35—64 CHAPTER II.
35—64 The Earliest History of the Indo-Aryan Family.
65—110 CHAPTER III.
65—79 Vaidik Theogony and Mythology.
79—88 Abstract Conceptions of the Deity.
88—91 Cosmogony.
91—98 Vaidik Doctrine of a Future Life.
98—104 Priesthood.
104—110 Vaidik Ceremonials of Worship.
111—140 CHAPTER IV.
111—123 The Division of the Vedas into Mantras and Brâhmaṇas.
123—127 The Proper Meaning of Sâkhâ, Charaṇa, and Parishad.
127—128 The Âraṇyakas.
128—139 The Upanishads.
139—140 The Distinction between Sruti and Smriti.
141—177 CHAPTER V.
141—143 The Peculiarities of the Sûtras.
143—157 The Vedângas.

157—158 The Origin and General Character of the
          Prâtiśâkhyas.
159—161 The Anukramaṇîs.
161—162 The Pariśishtas.
162—167 The Origin of Buddhism.
167—177 The Knowledge of Writing in ancient India.
179—189 APPENDIX.

A PEEP INTO THE VAIDIK AGE.

CHAPTER I.

General Character of the Vedas—the Vaidik Dialect and the Chronology of the Vaidik Age.

SIR William Jones said that the student of Indo-Aryan literature and religion found himself in the presence of infinity. The four Vedas, along with the other branches of literature closely connected with them, form a bulk so incredibly vast and of such enormous importance that not the whole body of sacred literature of any one ancient nation can compeer that of the Indo-Aryans. Our Aryan fathers handed to us the Vedas which in course of time have been canonized, and which notwithstanding many puerilities and repulsive legends, arrest our thoughts and inspire us with keen interest. Our heart grows warm when we find them to be replete with sober ideas, pure and sublime conceptions not unworthy of our most distant ancestors. In them we read the reflex of the laws and thoughts of a divine wisdom; and they are found to contain the thread which connects the present with the past. To the Vedas must be attached an undying interest and an ever increasing value not only for their great antiquity, but also for the immense flood of light which they throw on the primitive state of the Indo-Aryan society, Indo-Aryan speech and general mythology. We do not yet find in them any traces of a growing religion or a growing language; nevertheless we gain from them a real insight into the thoughts, the fears, the hopes, the doubts, and the faith of our ancestors. And in process of time the Vaidik religion, whatever it was, has become, through the corruptions and prejudices, of a most revolting type, of successive ages, a heterogeneous medley of theology, philosophy and science.

Beyond doubt, India claims a very high antiquity as well as a distinguished rank, among the civilised countries, of the ancient world. But unfortunately, there is no history* to record the heroic exploits of the Indo-Aryans, the word HISTORY being itself unknown in their language. Indeed, the Indo-Aryans never possessed any true 'historical sense'. However to get an insight into the state of the civilisation of the Vaidik age, it is necessary that we should refer to the pages

* Burnouf's History of Indian Buddhism, p. iii.

of the Vedas* themselves. The Vedas are the ancient Sástra of the Indo-Aryans, or as now they are called, the Hindus.†

The Vedas which stand at the head of the whole body of Indian literature, are altogether a peculiar class of writings. They are each, upon the whole, composed of the same identical matter; and they harmonise with one another in the external form and language, and in the nature of their contents. But when we take into consideration such other matters as are their special characteristics, the date and object of collection, and the adaptation of the hymns

---

* The word Veda is derived from the Sanskrit root vid to know, and is the same word as appears in the Greek Οἶδα, Latin video and vido, Gothic wait, Anglo-Saxon wát, and in the English wit; and may be translated knowing or knowledge.

† It is interesting to inquire into the origin of the term Hindu. It occurs with the whole treasure of Sanskrit words in the Sabda-kalpa-Druma, and therefore it may seem to many that it is of Sanskrit origin. But the authority which has been cited in it from the Merotantra, xxiii., to prove that it is such, shows, on the contrary, that it is a modern word. In fact, the Tantras are wanting in the halo of antiquity. The oldest among them, says Dr. Rájendralála Mitra, one of the most distinguished Sanskrit scholars in India, was not composed before the 3rd century of Christ, and the majority of them probably between the 6th and the 12th century. There is a word equivalent to the national name in the Zend. And it also re-appears as

to the ceremonial of worship, they respectively appear to be of an altogether dissimilar character. The Vedas are no less a repository of the songs with which our first ancestors addressed the gods in whom they believed, and extolled other matters with a spontaneous freshness and simplicity, than they are a store-house of also those songs which they had brought with them as the most precious heirlooms from their ancient homes. They consist, with a few exceptions, of detached prayers dedicated to divinities now no longer worshipped, some of whom are even entirely unknown. And in point of time and even in the progression of literary development they are probably the earliest existing literary records of the Hoddh for Hondû in a portion of the Hebrew scriptures called Esther. The term Hindu is not found to appear in any of the ancient Sanskrit authors. Indeed, this word has never been employed in the Sanskrit language. But nevertheless it is not of very modern origin. Herodotus (iv. 44; v. 3) has noticed the Hindus under the general appellation of Indoi. The word Hindu is derived from Sindhu; and the ancient Persians must have at first used the term, as it is established and it cannot be gainsaid, that according to Zend grammar the term Hindu traces its origin from Sindhu or Hindhu as they pronounced it. The Avestic Hapta-Heudu is nothing more than a transformation of the Sanskrit Sapta-Sindhavas. In the Cuneiform writings of the ancient Persians Hidds is used for Hindu, and it must be so understood.

Indo-Aryan race. The Vedas are four in number, viz., the Rig-veda—Veda of hymns, the Sáma-veda-Veda of chants, the Yajur-veda—Veda of sacrificial formulas, and the Atharva-veda—Veda of incantations. Manu, in his Institutes, often speaks of the three Vedas calling them *trayam brahma sanátanam*.* And Amara Sinha, in his Kosha, notices only three Vedas, and mentions the Atharvan without giving it the same designation. "The true reason why the three first Vedas are often mentioned without any notice of the fourth, must be sought, not in their different origin and antiquity, but in the difference of their use and purport."†

The Rig-veda is extant in two different recensions: one belonging to the Sákalas, and the other to the Váshkalas. Although the greater portion of the hymns of the Rik-Samhitá was composed on the banks of the Indus, their final redaction certainly took place in India proper during the period when the Brahmanical element had become predominant; and the Kosala-Videhas and the Kuru-Panchálas had the chief merit of having effected it. The Rik is to the student of history the Veda *par excellence*; it is the oldest of books and is the earliest depository

* Manu I. 23.
† Colebrooke's Essays, ed. Cowell, i. p. 11.

of Aryan faith. The Yajus and the Sáman presuppose the Rik; and the anteriority of the hymns to the Bráhmanas is proved not only by the frequent allusions to the former by the latter, but also by the words and phrases employed in the hymns themselves. The language and style of the Rik is artificial, and its poetry wants natural sublimity; but there is one redeeming feature in it namely that most of the hymns contain moral ideas and spiritual hopes and aspirations. Though there is little that is attractive and beautiful in the Rik, the volume itself gives life to antiquity and gives us a real and living idea of our early ancestors. As a complete panorama of ancient religion it reveals to us the very beginnings of human life and thought. Fortunately, however, there is no system or mythology in the Rik.

The Rik-Samhitá is a lyrical collection; and those lyrics are of the simplest form. We hardly find in it high flights of poetical fancy; and there is least trace of abstraction. And there is no doubt that this was composed in the infancy of the human race. As a real stratum of ancient thought and religion the Rik contains many things which are now quite unintelligible to us. The Rik contains some really historical elements; and Prof. Roth very justly calls it the historical Veda. Aufrecht remarks that possibly only a small portion of the Vaidik hymns may have been preserved to us in the Rik.* The Rik is evidently composed of heterogeneous materials. Its first seven books bear a similar character, arranged upon a like plan. These books comprehend the oldest, the most genuine and the most sacred hymns; and retain, as far as the tradition goes, an integral and not incongruous whole, and palpably remain as the Samhita was originally fixed and arranged. The eighth and ninth books present quite a different system of internal arrangement. The tenth book corresponds with the arrangement of two of its predecessors, and copiously supplies us with the most distinct evidences of a later origin. In various instances, the tradition is very unreliable with reference to their authorship, and even in certain cases attributes them to mythical personages.

The hymns are arranged in the order of the deities addressed, and in accordance to the families of rishi authors to which they are attributed. It is, therefore, probable, that the redaction of the text may have taken place at a later date than those of the Sâman and of the Yajus. The hymns are to be understood as combining the attributes of prayer and praise; and in them the goodness, the generosity,

* Weber's Indische Studien, iv. p. 8.

the power, the vastness, and even the personal beauty of the deities are described with no end of rhetorical flourish. And those deities are invoked to bestow blessings which are for the most part of a worldly and physical character; for food, wealth, life, posterity, cattle, cows and horses, protection against enemies, victory over them, and sometimes their destruction. The hymns themselves give no directions for their employment, and make no mention of the occasions on which they are to be applied, or of the ceremonies at which they are to be chanted.

Most of the hymns of the Rik-Samhitâ are found in the other Vedas, while none of their verses are to be met with in it. The fact that the hymns of the Sâman and the Yajus form part of the Rik, does not show that the contents of the latter were first brought together. The collecting together of the riches had to depend on other and more scientific causes. We may even suppose that science as usual, may have overdone her work; and instead of subjecting the ancient hymns to a considerable modification, may have rather improved upon them, and so transmitted to us a *rifacimento*.

We find in the Rik-Samhitâ some few hymns known by the name of *Khilas*, which were added at the end of a chapter after the whole collection of the ten books was completed. The *khilas*, as the Vaidik apocrypha, must be looked upon as a link closely connecting the Vaidik hymns with the later parts of Indo-Aryan literature. We can only accept them as successful imitations of the real and genuine songs, but as such they have acquired a certain degree of sanctity. They gradually crept into the Samhitás of the other Vedas; they are referred to in the Bráhmanas, although they are not counted in the Anukramanis. There is another class of hymns called *dánastutis* or praises of certain kings for their gifts to the priests. These hymns bear, on the whole, a modern character, and they possibly belong to the Mantra period.

The *Rik-Samhitá* is certainly a wonderful work, and attests the existence of a scientific development of mind among the Indo-Aryans at a time long before the age of the poems of Homer or Hesiod. It must not be assumed that the hymns of this Veda are altogether of a religious character. A hymn in the seventh book recounts in a singularly jocular manner the revival of the frogs at the commencement of the rains, and likens their croaking to the singing of the Brahmans in ceremonious worship. Again, in the tenth book we have the lamentation of a gamester over his ruinous devotion to play. Numerous other instances might be easily adduced. In all probability those portions, which must be regarded as non-religious, belong to a later period.

The hymns of the *Rik* themselves are apparently of different periods, some being older and some more recent;[a] but we have no data to determine their relative antiquity. The older and the more recent hymns are so distinguished by their language and style on the one hand, and their conception on the other. They are drawn up in a great variety of metres, most of which are peculiar to them. The metres so employed show a long and successful cultivation of rhythmical contrivance. We find

---

[a] i. 12, 11; i. 27, 4; i. 60, 3; i. 89, 9; i. 96, 2; i. 130, 10; i. 143, 1; ii. 17, 1; ii. 24, 1; iii. 1. 20; vi. 17, 13; vi. 22, 7; vi. 44, 13; vi. 48, 11; vi. 50, 6. Max Müller designates the most ancient portion of the hymns by the term *chhandas*, and those that are comparatively modern, *mantra* (see his History of Ancient Sanskrit Literature, pp. 70, 525 ff). But it is to be observed that he is altogether singular in the use of these two words in the above sense, as it nowhere obtains in Sanskrit books. Besides the Brâhmaṇa portion all the rest is called *mantra*. In the Purusha-Sûkta even the metrical portion of the Yajus is characterized as *chhandas*, and this is also proved by a text of the Atharvan (xi. 7, 24). Pâṇini in his Grammar repeatedly speaks of the Vedas in the term of *chhandas*. *Chhandas* is a term indicating sometimes the *mantra* portion, and sometimes even the Brâhmaṇa portion (Goldstücker's Pâṇini, p. 71). In the entire collection of ancient and modern

the technical names of some metres mentioned in the later portion of the Rik. It is beyond doubt that such a large national collection as the Rik-Samhitā could never have been composed by the men of one or even two generations; and it is to be especially observed here that it contains the hymns of the sons as well as the hymns of their fathers and earlier ancestors.* This acknowledgment constitutes one of the historical elements in the Veda. It is an acknowledgment on their part that numerous persons had existed, and a series of events occurred long before their own age. It is possible that several centuries must have elapsed between the composition of the oldest and that of the most recent richas; and in this intervening period the Indo-Aryan community passed through various

works in Sanskrit, *chhandas* is exclusively applied to the whole body of the Vedas. But *chhandas* is nowhere employed for the ancient portions of the Vedas nor useful for those that are comparatively modern. Müller further considers that Sanskrit *chhandas* and Avestic Zand are both equivalent terms. Although they appear to resemble in sound and letter, yet there is nothing of affinity in signification. Zand means language or translation; while *chhandas* means the original Vedas.

* i. 1, 2; i. 48, 14; i. 118, 8; i. 131, 6; iv. 50, 1; vi. 21, 1; vi. 22, 2; vii. 53, 1; vii. 76, 4; ix. 110, 7; x. 14, 15.

stages of development, either social, moral, religious or intellectual.

The first book of the Rik-Samhitá contains one hundred and ninety-one hymns which are with some exceptions, ascribed to fifteen different authors such as Gotama, Kanva, Kutsa, Sunahsepa, Kakshivan, Agastya, &c. The second containing forty-three hymns is attributed to Gritsamada ; the third, sixty-two, to Viswámitra ; the fourth, fifty-eight, to Vámadeva ; the fifth, eighty-seven, to Atri ; the sixth, seventy-five, to Bharadvája ; the seventh, one hundred and four, to Vasishtha ; the eighth, ninety-two, (besides 11 Válkhilya-súktas) to Kanva ; the ninth, one hundred and fourteen, to Angiras ; and the tenth, one hundred and ninety-one, to Rishis of different families and also to mythical personages. The names of the authors are given here ; but by those names we must understand also their families. The súktas or hymns again are distinguished by different names, as Mahá-súkta, Kshudra-súkta, Madhyam-súkta, Rishisúkta, Devatá-súkta, and Chhandah-súkta ; and these terms are applied simply to designate certain scientific arrangements of the entire mass of the súktas specially with reference to the deity, author, metre, and the quantity of richas of each of them. The worship which we find in the hymns of the Rik must have consisted more of isolated sacrificial ceremonials than of a series of acts constituting an elaborate sacrifice. Yet there are various other hymns, which indicate the existence, at their time, of highly complex and artificial rituals. It does not therefore follow that the Rik as such, was drawn up for the purpose of being sung at their performances.

The Sâma-veda is an anthology, and purely a derivative production. It is nothing more than a recast of the Rik, being composed, with some exceptions, of the very same hymns, which are in their rich-form, although with the sâman-accents. The Sâma-Samhitâ has come down to us in two recensions: one of which belongs to the school of the Rânâyanîyas, and the other to that of the Kauthumas. These recensions on the whole differ very little from each other. The Sâman consists of two parts; the A'rchika and Staubhika. The A'rchika is composed of five hundred and eighty-five verses, of which five hundred and thirty-nine are taken from the Rik; and as adapted to the general and frequent use of the priests, exists in two forms, called Gânas, the Grâmageya-gâna (erroneously called Veya-gâna) which is divided into seventeen prapâthakas; and the A'ranya-gâna into six prapâthakas. The Staubhika contains twelve hundred and twenty-three verses, of which eleven hundred and ninety-four are borrowed from the Rik. This portion exists in the same manner in two forms, called the Uha-gâna which is divided into twenty-three prapâthakas; and the Uhya-gâna into six prapâthakas. The Sâman among other Vedas has a peculiar feature of its own in as much as it is provided with a system of accents which consist of no less than ten different signs. The chief object of this collection must have been, as it appears from its special characteristics that its *richas* should be chanted during the ceremonies of Soma offering and on different other ceremonial occasions. The inference that the modern origin of some of the hymns of the Rik can be proved by their not occurring in the Sâman, has been well and ably refuted by Dr. Portsch.

Prof. Benfey has shown in the preface (p. xix.) to his valuable edition of the Sâma-Samhita that there are in it some verses, the absence of which in the Rik is conspicuous. The total absence of seventy-one verses found in the recension of the Sâman, from the recension in which we now possess the Rik-Samhita, must be accounted for by the circumstance, that these verses belonged to one or the other of the recensions of the Rik, which are altogether lost. The relation of the Sâman with the

Rik is to a certain degree analogous to that between the White and the Black Yajus.* The Sâman and the Yajus are the attendants of the Rik.† The hymns in the Sâman exhibit not a single sign of having been enlarged from the original size: the Yajus, however, has considerably extended. Both show different readings varying in greater or less degree from those of the Rik-Samhitâ. The *richas* occurring in the Sâma-Samhitâ and Yajuh-Samhitâ are, with a few exceptions, borrowed in an altered form from the Rik-Samhitâ; and they present very little harmony with the text of the latter. But the *richas* found in the Sâman are to be taken as older and more original on account of the greater antiquity of their grammatical forms than those of the two Samhitâs of the Yajus. Some of the Sûtras of the Sâman are little more than lists, such as we find in the Anukramanîs, appended to the other Vedas. Their style, on the whole, very nearly approaches the style of the Sûtra works.

The Yajur-veda is in double form; the Black and White Yajus. These, in the main, have the same matter; but they differ from each other only as regards their arrangement. In the Black Yajus

* Weber's Indische Studien, i. p. 68 ff.
† Kaushîtakî-Brâhmana, vi. 11 : तदुहरिवर्चा वियदी वेदी ।

the formulas for the entire sacrificial ceremonial are generally accompanied by their dogmatical explanations, and ritual supplements; while in the White Yajus the case is quite different, there they form subjects that are entirely distinct from one another. The Black Yajus is the older of the two; the White embraces texts which are not found in the Black, and viewed in reference to the motley character of the former, it looks 'white,' or orderly. The Black and the White Yajus originated, no doubt, with a schism of which Yájnavalkya was most probably the author. They originated in the eastern parts of Hindustan, in the country of the Kurupanchálas, and they belong to a period when the Brahmanical organisation, and the system of caste were completely consolidated.* Three different recensions of the Black Yajus is known to us; one that of Á'pastamba, a sub-division of the Khándikíyas; the other, the Káṭhaka, which belongs to the school of the Charakas; and another the Á'treya, a sub-division of the Aukhíyas. The Samhitá of the Black Yajus is in fact a medley of undigested fragments of all sorts. It consists of seven books; these again, are divided into forty-four prasnas, six hundred and fifty-one anuvákas, and two thousand, one hundred and ninety-

* Weber's History of Indian Literature, p. 10.

eight kandikâs. The recensions of the White Yajus bear the names of the Kanvas and of the Mâdhyamdinas. In both the recensions it consists of forty adhyâyas; but in the Mâdhyamdina recension these are again sub-divided into three hundred and three anuvâkas, and one thousand, nine hundred and seventy-five kandikâs. And the redaction of the Yajus was accomplished by the Kuru-Panchâlas and the Kosala-Videhas when they were in their prime.

The Yajuh-Samhitâ consists principally of prayers and invocations to be used at the consecration of utensils and at sacrificial ceremonials. The origin of the Yajus is precisely like that of the Sâman; but the paraphernalia of the equally complicated and highly developed ritual for which the compilation of this Veda became necessary is more elaborate and more attractive than that of the Sâman. The Indo-Aryans looked with special preference on the Yajus, for it could better satisfy their sacrificial wants than the Sâman or the Rik. "The Yajurveda," says Sâyana, in his Introduction to the Taittirîya-Samhitâ, "is like a wall, the two other Vedas like paintings (on it)." The history of the Yajuh-Samhitâ differs palpably enough from that of the other Vedas, in that it is characterized by a disagreement between its own schools, which is far more weighty than the dissensions which widened the gulf between the schools of the different Vedas. These schools are founded on a division of the Yajuh-Samhita; the one party adhering to what is called the Black Yajus; and the other to the White Yajus. And there is strong reason to suppose that the division must have happened even after the time of Panini.* Some commentators explain sukla or 'white' by suddha.† The White Yajus is attributed to Yájnavalkya, and the Black Yajus to Tittiri.

The Atharva-veda, though next after the Rik, is the most comprehensive and valuable of the two other collections. This is not exactly a Veda, although many of the hymns or incantations of which it is composed, appear to be of great antiquity.‡ It was but after a hard struggle that the Atharvan came off victorious, and at last took the rank as a fourth Veda. Passages of the sacred scriptures themselves seem to support the inference that the Atharvan is not exactly a Veda, as it is not mentioned in the passage

* Goldstücker's Pāṇini, p. 130 ff.

† Dvivedaganga explains शुक्लानि यजूंषि by शुक्लानि वर मङ्गलानिचिन्तनीयानि ।

‡ See, on the subject of this Veda, Müller's Ancient Sanskrit Literature, pp. 28, 446 ff.; Weber's History of Indian Literature, p. 10.; and Prof. Whitney's papers in the Journal of the American Oriental Society, iii. 305 ff.; and iv. 254 ff.

cited from the White Yajus Mr. Colebrooke in his essay on Religious Ceremonies.* It is more like an historical than a liturgical collection. The greater portion of the Atharvan is to be found in the last book of the *Rik-Samhitâ*.† The extant Samhitâ belongs to the school of the Saunakas, and to the period when Brahmanism had become dominant. There was, however, a Samhitâ belonging to the Paippalâda school. But the variations that occur in the former are so prominent that a learned writer calls them "capricious inversions and alterations."‡ This collection, however, appears to consist of complete hymns and not of single unconnected verses; and its internal arrangement is authentic. In this respect it is akin to the *Rik*, and can be properly called a complement of the first Veda, a complement containing the store of hymns suited to its time. The Atharvan is divided into twenty kândas and thirty-eight prapâthakas consisting nearly of seven hundred and sixty hymns, and of about six

* Asiatic Researches, vii. p. 251.

† "By the followers of the Atharvan, the richas, or stanzas of the *Rig-veda*, are numerously included in their own Sanhitâ (or collection)."—Sâyanâchâryn, Introduction, Müller's edition, p. 2.

‡ Roth on the Literature and History of the Vedas.

hundred verses. Besides the division into prapāṭhakas, there is another into anuvākas; of which there are some ninety. This Veda, perhaps, on account of the mystery which shrouds its songs, gained not a small degree of holiness, which even surpassed that of the older Vedas. From the Atharvanrahasya it appears that the three other Vedas enable a man to fulfil the dharma, or religious law; but the Atharvan helps him to attain moksha, or eternal beatitude.

The Atharva-Samhitā is rather a supplement than one of the four Vedas, and has very little coincidence with others in its general character, or in its style. It marks off the intermediate period of transition from the simple faith of the early times to the gross superstition of the subsequent period. It is not however so much of priestly as of popular origin; and its language conclusively proves a different and later era. Its most peculiar feature consists not so much in the fact that it contains matters quite of a dissimilar character from that of the other Vedas, as in the fact that it comprises a great number of incantations. The Atharvan contains formulas supposed to have the influence of protecting against injurious influences of the divine powers, with imprecations on enemies, prayers against diseases and noxious animals, as well as for the efficacy of healing herbs, for protection in travelling, luck in play, and such like things. The first eighteen books of the Samhita, with which it was originally drawn up, are arranged upon one system throughout. A sixth of the bulk not metrical, but consists of longer or shorter prose pieces, which tally, in point of language and style, with the passages of the Brâhmanas. As regards the authorship tradition does not afford any valuable information; but they are with some exceptions ascribed to fictitious personages.

The Vedas do not appear to be the productions of one and the same author or even of the same age.*

* It seems strange that one so well informed as Max Müller should have published the following sentences: "In the most ancient Sanskrit literature, the idea even of authorship is excluded. Works are spoken of as revealed to and communicated by certain sages, but not as composed by them." *History of Ancient Sanskrit Literature*, p. 523. The earlier Rishis did not in any case lay claim to inspiration; but they knew and believed themselves to be simply the authors of the Vedas, and not to be writing by inspiration from God, as it has been alleged. They appear to have distinctly described themselves as the composers of the hymns. The verbs which they employed to express this idea are kri, "to make" (i. 184, 5; ii. 30, 8; iii. 30, 20; iv. 6, 11; vi. 52, 2; vii. 31, 14; viii. 51, 4; viii.

"At whatever time the work of collection may have been performed, it was decidedly an era in the history of Indian literature: from this time the texts became the chief object of the science and industry 79, 3; x. 54, 6; x. 101, 2); *taksh*, "to fabricate" = the Greek τεκταίνομαι (i. 62, 13; i. 130, 6; ii. 19, 8; ii. 35, 2; v. 2, 11; v. 29, 15; vi. 32, 1; vii. 7, 6; viii. 6, 53; x. 39, 14; x. 80, 7); and *jan* "to beget," or "produce" (iii. 2, 1; vii. 15, 4; vii. 22, 9; viii. 43, 2; viii. 77, 4; viii. 84, 4, 5; ix. 78, 2; x. 4, 1). Nevertheless the Rishis seem to have attached a high value to their productions, which, to their belief, were acceptable to the gods (v. 45, 4; v. 55, 1; vii. 26, 1, 2; x. 23, 6; x. 54, 6; x. 105, 8). There are also passages in the Rik which ascribe a supernatural character to the earlier Rishis, (vii. 76, 4; iii. 53, 9; vii. 23, 11 ff; vii. 87, 4; vii. 88, 3 ff; x. 14, 15; x. 62, 4, 5); and even to the hymns (i. 37, 4; vii. 34, 1; vii. 34, 9; x. 176, 2). And the Rishis are said to have held conversation about sacred truths with the gods (i. 179, 2). Again, some among them professed their ignorance of all matters either human or divine (i. 164, 5). When the idea of inspiration and of independent composition is traceable in all the parts of the Rik-Samhitâ, it is possible that the notion of inspiration may not have occupied the minds of the earlier sages; but may have grown up among their successors, or more properly that it may have been entertained by some and not by all of them. The Indian authors shortly before, or subsequent to, the collection of the Vaidik hymns held the opinions on the origin of the Vedas, as springing from the mystical sacrifice of Purusha, Rig-veda, x. 9; as resting on of the nation; as they had always been of its highest reverence and admiration; and so thorough and religious was the care bestowed upon their preservation that, notwithstanding their mass and the thousands of years which have elapsed since their collection, not a single various reading, so far as is yet known, has been suffered to make its way into them. The Skambha, *Atharva-veda*, x. 7, 14; as springing from Indra, xiii. 4, 33; as produced from time, xix. 54, 3; as produced from Agni, Vāyu, and Sūrya, *Manu*, i. 23, and *Satapatha-Brāhmaṇa*, xi. 5, 8, 1 ff.; as springing from Prajāpati and the waters, *Satapatha-Brāhmaṇa*, vi. 1, 1, 8; as springing from the leavings of the sacrifice (uchchhishṭa), *Atharva-veda*, xi. 7, 24; as issued from the mouth of Brahmā at the creation, *Vishṇu-Purāṇa*, i. 5, 48 ff., *Bhāgavata-Purāṇa*, iii. 12, 34 and 37 ff., and *Mārkaṇḍeya-Purāṇa*, 102, 1; as created by Brahmā, or as produced from the Gāyatrī, *Harivaṃsa*, verses 47, and 11, 516; as created by Vishṇu, or as having Sarasvatī for their mother, *Mahābhārata*, *Sāntiparva*, verse 12, 920, etc. etc. In like manner, many other authorities might be produced to the same effect, but how those opinions are puerile and contradictory in themselves. The Hindus designated the older hymns, and the more recent ones by various names, such as *arka*, *gāthā*, *rich*, *gir*, *dhī*, *nītha*, *nīvid*, *mantra*, *sūti*, *sūkta*, *stoma*, *vach*, *vachas*, *sāman*, *yajus*, *manman*, *manīshā*, *sumati*, *dhīti*, *dhishaṇā*, *stuti*, *stava*, *sushṭuti*, *praśasti*, etc. etc.; and they also often applied to them the title of *brahma* which has the sense of hymn or prayer.

influence which they have exerted upon the whole literary development of after ages is not easily to be rated too high."*

All that is not found of the oldest Veda in the Sâman and Yajus, is a Rik piece-meal; its hymns broken into parts; verses from different hymns arranged anew, and even the composition of numerous parts brought into the same songs, as if they had the same author. That under such treatment, the Yajus should have lost all worth as far as poetry is concerned, was only to be expected; it is, however, a curious fact, that the Sâman should have preserved so much, as it even now does, of that beauty which marks so peculiarly the Rig-veda poetry. The Atharvan, too, is composed in a like way as the Yajus, with only some variants, that the additions in it to the mutilated extracts from the Rik are more considerable than those in the Yajus.

There exists no record that carries us back to a more primitive state of the human family than the Rig-veda. And so the few relics that have been preserved to us, are of most intense interest. It has been very appropriately said that there is one oasis in the vast desert of ancient Asiatic history, and it is the only real Veda, the Rig-veda, the oldest book

*Journal of the American Oriental Society, iii. p. 309.

in the Aryan world. The priority of the Rik to all the other Vedas is thoroughly established by the fact that its numerous hymns are found in them, and that its Rishis are referred to in the Atharvan. In the Atharvan the names so produced, are principally of the more recent Rishis, while those in the Rik are of a more ancient time.* In the Atharvan a more developed state of the institutions together with the caste system appears than what we find in the Rik. In the former we see the people bound hand and foot by the fetters of the hierarchy and superstition, while in the latter we find them quite free, and imbued with a warm love for nature. Judging from the language and internal character of the Atharvan, we arrive at the conclusion that the main body of this Veda was in existence at a time when the Rik was compiled. In the Yajus Samhitâ an enumeration is given of the different classes of men who are to be consecrated at the Purusha-medha, and of the names of most of the mixed castes. We may, therefore, conclude that the Brahmanical element had then gained the supremacy, and the system of caste was completely organized.

The 90th hymn of the tenth book of the Rig-

* Muth, Literature and History of the Vedas, p. 15.

c

veda is entitled the Purusha-Sûkta, which is found also in the 31st book of the Vâjasaneyi-Samhitâ, and in the 19th book of the Atharva-veda. The fact that the Sâman has not any verse extracted from it, is not without meaning. The opening parts of the Sûkta are of a pantheistic character; and the whole of it contains allusions to the sacrificial ceremonials, and not to the actual immolation of a human victim. In it the sacrifice is not offered to the gods but by the gods themselves. Nor are there human priests mentioned, and the Purusha could not have been an ordinary man. It is full of technical and philosophical terms; and contains certain modern words such as Sûdra, Rajanya; and there is also mention of the three seasons the spring, summer and autumn, which does not occur in the other hymns. From these facts it is apparent that it belongs to the close of the Vaidik age; and it is found scarcely to enunciate any uniform, orthodox and authoritative doctrine in regard to the four-fold origin of the human race.

Different parts of the Rik-Samhita were composed by different Rishis. Each hymn is said to have had its Rishi; and these Rishis comprise a variety of secular as well as religious individuals, who are celebrated at different eras in Indian tradition. The pristine traditions, though few, are yet sufficient

(27)

to prove that in the Vaidik age the capacity for metrical composition, and the highest prerogative of officiating at the services of the gods, were not regarded as exclusively confined to individuals of priestly caste. Even females are spoken of as authors of hymns or parts of hymns, as Romasā, daughter of Brihaspati (i. 126), Lopamudrā (i. 179. 1), and Visvavārā, of the family of Atri (v. 28). And it is also a very remarkable and curious fact that we find one Kavasha Ailūsha, himself a Sūdra, to have composed a few of the Sūktas in the tenth book of the Rig-veda. The epithets applied by the authors of the hymns to themselves and to the sages who in earlier times had appointed, as well as to their contemporaries who followed them in conducting, the different rites at the services of the gods, are the following: *rishi, kavi, medhāvin, vipra, vipaschit, vedhas, muni,* etc. The Vedas are said to have been perpetuated by tradition, until they were arranged in their present order by Krishna Dvaipāyana Vyāsa, the Indian Pisistratus.* Vyāsa, who flourished in the early part of the twelfth century B. C.,† having

* Lassen's Indian Antiquities, i. p. 777, note, and also Mahábhárata, l. 2417 and 4236.

† Archdeacon Pratt's Letter on Colebrooke's Determination of the Date of the Vedas, in the Journal of the Asiatic Society of

compiled and arranged the so-called revealed scriptures of the Indo-Aryans, taught them to several of his disciples, viz., the Rik to Paila, the Yajus to Vaisampayna, the Saman to Jaimini, and the Atharvan to Sumanta.

The Vedas are written in an ancient form of Sanskrit which is to the later what Chaucer's writings are to modern English. They abound in obsolete and peculiar formations, made up of the more recent grammatical forms with so much irregularity as lead to the inference that the language was too unsettled and variable to be brought under subjection to a system of rigid grammatical rules.

The Vaidik dialect is to be understood as the least altered representative of that original tongue from which are descended the languages of the leading races of Asia and Europe. The dialect of the first three Vedas is very ancient and at the same time very difficult. When it is compared with the classical Sanskrit it appears that both are phonetically and grammatically almost the same, but lexically they are as wide as possible.

The chronology of the Vaidik age is indicated in the different styles of composition of the Vedas, the

Bengal, 1862, p. 52; and Journal of the American Oriental Society, viii. pp. 83, 84.

Brâhmanas and the Sûtras. The Vaidik age is divided into four distinct periods: namely the Chhandas period, the Mantra period, the Brâhmana period, and the Sûtra period. The respective styles of composition of these four periods differ very much from each other. The Chhandas period furnishes us with a fair picture of the early society of the Indo-Aryans at a time when no particular system of religion was prevalent. Sacrifices were not then in vogue. But in the Mantra period they were held in great estimation. The Brâhmana period gave birth to the Brahmans. In this period, theological speculations were much indulged in. The Vedas have their own Brâhmanas and Sûtras; and when the Sûtras pre-suppose the Brâhmanas, and the Brâhmanas do not refer to them, it is proved that the Brâhmana period must have preceded the Sûtra period. Lastly in the Sûtra period, commentaries on the Vedas and Upanishads were prepared. About this time the Sanskrit language underwent important modifications. We can place the Sûtra period in the middle of the Vaidik and Paurânika ages, forming a period in which occurred one of the most remarkable changes in the Indo-Aryan religion and society.

The Chhandas period may be supposed, according to some scholars, to have lasted from 1200 to 1000

B. C.; the Mantra period from 1000 to 800 B. C.; the Brâhmana period from 800 to 600 B. C.; and the Sûtra period extending from 600 to 200 B. C. "To decide the question," says Barthélémy Saint-Hilaire, "with absolute certainty as to the dates of these four periods of ancient Sanskrit literature, would be impossible; for Indian literature itself is almost without known dates, owing either to the peculiar organisation of the Hindu mind, or to the convulsions of Indian society. The present condition of Sanskrit philology does not afford the scholar the requisite data for embarking with any chance of success in such chronological speculations. Uncertainty hangs over these periods; and to assign an approximate length to each of these periods is altogether hazardous. It should be well understood that these dates are only approximately accurate, and notwithstanding the apparent accuracy of the figures, it is clear that one cannot in this case arrive at any precise determination. Moreover Max Müller would perhaps have done better, if he had not sought to fix such precise limits to write down the result of his investigations so accurately. As there is necessarily always much vagueness in calculations of this nature, it is well that the form given to hypothesis be just as vague as our data; and as there is nothing so certain as a number once pronounced, I think it would have been better to remain partly in the dark, which in fact, is quite excusable in such matters. Besides, every body will see that the chronological limits assigned by Max Müller to the four periods of Vaidik literature are too narrow rather than too wide. The same conviction has been expressed by Professor Wilson, and Dr. Whitney. If Max Müller is wanting in any thing it is chiefly through an excess of reserve. The period of the Samhitás, such as we now possess, is dated at least 1000 years before the Christian era. One may, without the slightest hesitation, place the period of Chhandas far beyond that. Then again one alights upon the calculations of Sir William Jones, and of Colebrooke, who assigned to the composition of the Rig-veda a period 14 or 15 hundred years before Christ.

In another point of view, this uniform length of two centuries assigned to the period of the Bráhmanas, as well as to that of the Mantras and of Chhandas, is equally liable to criticism. If the period of the Sútras, comprised four entire centuries, it seems scarcely probable that the period of the Bráhmanas which are just as long and perhaps equally numerous, should not have extended over a longer time, including the Âranyakas and the Upanishads. Moreover there is certainly a far smaller interval between the Brâhmanas and the Sûtras, than there is between the Mantras and the Brâhmanas. Nevertheless Max Müller reckons only two centuries between each of these two classes. Analogy would seem to authorize the assumption of a far longer interval between the latter than between the former. There is an immense difference between the period assigned to the collection of sacred poetry, and the period in which they are commented upon; there is a smaller difference between this latter epoch and the one in which these manifold and obscure commentaries are reduced to clear and orderly rules. As for the period of the Mantras, it seems in its turn too extensive, if that of the Brâhmanas is not sufficiently so. Granted that two centuries had been necessary for the composition of the Brâhmanas, the simple collection of the Samhitâs did not require so much time. Thus, without contesting the absolute length of the united periods, their relative length does not seem to be very acceptable, and their proportions might be settled in a totally different manner, which could be equally justified. As for the period of the Chhandas, the first of all, and the most fertile, since it has rendered all the rest comparatively worthless, it is to be presumed that it was the longest, and this inspiration, which, during more than three thousand years has enlivened the entire religious creed of a great people, cannot have been of so short a duration, since its effects are so durable."

First the hymns were composed, and then the Brâhmanas. It is therefore possible that several centuries intervened between the composition of both the hymns and the Brâhmanas as a not inconsiderable space of time must have required for the literal sense of the hymns becoming somewhat obscure, and invested with a halo of sacredness. In the same manner the period during which the Brâhmanas were drawn up must have been separated by several centuries as a sufficient space of time must have elapsed for further modification of language, and the growth of a new theology which claimed for the Brâhmanas the same sacredness which the Brâhmanas themselves did for the hymns. There are however no sufficient data by which we can determine with precision the period during which the hymns were composed. The hymns are divided into two classes, the Mantras or more recent hymns which according to some scholars may have been produced as between 1000 and 800 years as has been said before; and the Chhandas or the older hymns which, they suppose, may have been composed as between 1200-1000 B. C. Other scholars hold altogether a different opinion; and that opinion is shared by Dr. Haug who thus writes: "We do not hesitate therefore, to assign the composition of the bulk of the Brâhmaṇas to the year 1400-1200 B. C.; for the Samhitâ we require a period of *at least* 500-600 years, with an interval of about two hundred years between the end of the proper Brâhmaṇa period. Thus we obtain for the bulk of Samhitâ the space from 1400-2000 B.C.; the oldest hymns and sacrificial formulas may be a few hundred years more ancient still, so that we would fix the very commencement of Vaidik literature between 2000-2400 B. C."* However there are no mile-stones in Vaidik literature. The classification of ancient Sanskrit literature has now become a theme for discussion by every Sanskrit scholar. But where it is to end is not easy to surmise. It has been questioned whether the basis of that classification is scientific or ritual or theological. But whatever may be advanced against such an arrangement, I have every reason to place my faith in the distribution of Vaidik literature into four distinct periods.

* Haug's Introduction to the Aitareya-Brâhmaṇa, p. 47.

CHAPTER II.

The Earliest History of the Indo-Aryan Family.

Media was probably the earliest centre of ethnic radiation, the homestead of the human family, the ancestral abode of those races which have hitherto guided the van of civilization. The languages and mythologies of almost all the great historic races, however now widely separated, beckon to that country. Amidst the recesses of that focus of movement and cradle of historic races, lie the materials of forty centuries of human history. When such dubious half-blind guides as mythology and tradition fail to penetrate into what lie in the pre-historic deeps the languages can only with scientific certainty point out. So comparative Philology has been very justly called linguistic Palæontology. A study of the morphology and grammar of the Sanskrit in its oldest form, and of those of the Celtic, Greek, Latin, Lettish, Slavonic and Persian languages, shows us that all these languages have descended from one original speech. It follows therefore as necessary corollary that the nations who spoke the languages were themselves also descended from one and the same stock, and they constituted one united people. Affinity in language affords some presumption of affinity in race; but language is not the only respect in which an affinity exists between the Indians, Iranians, Greeks, and Romans; their mythologies also imply a community of origin, and they yield some data for ethnic deductions. At any rate, the cradle of the Aryans is to be sought for in some country external to India; and the facts which have been brought to light enable us to determine the region in which our ancestors must have lived together.

The pre-emigration events as recorded in the Rig-veda, which again are confirmed by the Zand Avesta and the Assyrian Inscriptions, and by a legend in the Satapatha-Brâhmana, naturally point to the westward of Asia for the primitive home of the Aryans; and also to their migratory path from "the West to the East." Our ancestors as well speak of their "old home," the *pratna okas;** but cannot give its geography. However, this admission on their part shows clearly that they came to India from beyond the Indus; and moreover the testimonies which have been brought to light point to Media as that home. Afterwards a Turanian invasion of the country was probably the

* Rig-Veda, i. 80, 9.

cause of their dispersion on all sides. It is not easy to define their routes; some went westward, others eastward. But probably those that came eastward had to encounter on their way the conflicts which are recorded in the Vedas and the Zend Avesta; and this is also corroborated by the temporary disappearance of Vishnu from them. Their marches were something like religious processions; regularly worshipping and performing their ceremonial acts, the rear and flank guards repeating hymns in the Vaidik seven metres,* and the vanguard bearing the holy fire in the front.† Some of them may have remained behind, and settled in the different directions of their route. Those that went westward were the first to leave their pristine home; and those that came eastward were the last. And probably after many defections in the course of their migration the latter made a settlement which they called the Airyana-Vaëjo which was at a great distance beyond the Jaxartes. In the Rig-veda an expression also occurs from which we might infer that the Indo-Aryans still retained some recollection of their having at one time occupied a colder country.‡ And in the

* Rig-veda, i. 22, 16.
† Muir's Sanskrit Texts, iv. 107.
‡ Rig-veda, i. 64, 14; vi. 4, 8; vi. 10, 7; vi. 12, 6; vi. 13.

allusions made to the Uttarakurus there may be some reminiscence of an early connexion with the countries to the north of the Himálayas.* Ptolemy (vi. 16) was also acquainted with the Uttarakurus. According to Lassen the Ottorokora (οττοροκόρα) of Ptolemy must be sought for to the east of Kashghar. In the Airyana-Vaêjo they continued to form one community even after the other kindred tribes had estranged from them; and to live on equal terms so far as the worship of the sun and fire and the elements of Nature was concerned. They also tolerated and practised the primitive institution of sacrifices; though they differed as to their scope and the mode of conducting them. But one party insisted on the actual completion of the sacrifice as the *Vashat*; while the other would not allow it. Nor would the latter sanction even the use of the Soma drink by which the former set store. There were some principal doctrinal differences between both the parties; and such religious differences only separated the one from the other.† And both the parties latterly formed again two other branches, the Indo-Aryans and the Iranians. Now each branch bore

6 ; vi. 17, 15.
* Aitareya-Brâhmana, viii. 14.
† Bleeck, Introduction to the Avesta, p. x.

feelings of bitterness to the other; and many were the sanguinary conflicts which took place between them. It also appears from the Rig-Veda that Ishtâsva or Vistaspa of the Zand Avesta, who was the patron of Zoroaster,* had contemplated the forcible imposition of his prophet's teaching on the whole Aryan family. But the ancestors of the Indo-Aryans refused manfully to submit to such religious intolerance; and they strenuously defended their own religion. "What can Ishtâsva," said they, "what can Ishtarasmi, rulers of the world as they are, do against our protecting men?"†

Media was probably the *officina gentium* whence issued swarms of men whose descendants now constitute the most civilized nations of the earth; and the migration of those men belongs to a period far beyond the reach of documentary history. After crossing the narrow passes of the Hindukush, the Indo-Aryans first settled on the north-western frontiers of India, in the Panjab, and they gradually spread towards the east, beyond the Sarasvatî, and over Hindustan as far as the Ganges. Many centuries were necessarily required to subjugate the wild and

* In the Rig-veda (vii. 37, 7) this name appears in the corrupt form of Jaradashti.

† Rig-veda, i. 122, 13.

vigorous aborigines, to break down their residences, and to bring them over to Brahmanism. The Indo-Aryans so isolated themselves from their primitive settlement as to have lost in a very short time all sympathy for their cousins. And after they had got a home in India, they began also to ignore all trans-Indus events, and to declare themselves as the autochthones of Indian soil. In India they must have established themselves by household groups, each occupying a specifically assigned area within the boundaries of which the intruders were only allowed to settle upon terms of subjection. Though bound together by the feelings of a common descent, language and religion, and by their joint hostility to the aborigines, they were divided into clans quite separate from one another. They were now communities of free men. In such a state the position of an individual member was as the head of a family and the master of wealth. Now they stood in constant alarm of the aborigines; and they were often engaged in hostilities with them, and even with the members of their own community, simply with a view to be enriched with the booty. The country now occupied was partly cultivated, and partly covered by forests. And it was no doubt peopled by various tribes, and divided into numerous principalities.

At such primitive times when they were all a pastoral and agricultural people, there could exist no distinct caste of cultivators of the earth; when they were all warriors there could be no military caste; and when each member of the community had the privilege to approach to the gods with their own prayers and offerings there could be no sacerdotal order. Then the castes had no existence. At the time when the Indo-Aryans left their original home, and set foot on Indian soil, they naturally came into contact with the Dasyus or the aborigines of India. These people, forming the Turanian branch of the human family, differed widely from the Indo-Aryans, in their physical appearance and color, language and manners. Under such divergence, there was no ground for the establishment or conservation of feelings of amity and unity between the classes. Consequently, the Indo-Aryans and the Dasyus frequently found themselves in the bitterest conflict. The Indo-Aryans, as they were naturally of fair complexion, of majestic appearance, civilized and much more advanced in thought, looked down upon the aborigines who were of beastly appearance. In the Vedas, the aborigines are frequently called Dasyus or Dâses;* and the Indo-Aryans, with a certain

* Rig-veda, I. 12, 4.

(42)

degree of hatred, called them *krishnatachara*.* From the Vedas, we obtain sufficient evidence of there having been a wide difference and natural enmity between them; and the Indo-Aryans are found scornfully to apply to the Dasyus the terms of *avrata*, *apavrata*, *ayajyu*, *abrahma*, *adeva*, *anindra*, etc.† The main difference consisted only in color and feature, and hence *varna* gradually came to imply caste. Caste then was purely an ethnological institution. In the Veda *varna* appears in the sense of color (i. 73, 7; i. 113, 2), of bright color or light (iii. 34, 5), and of race, the white and the dark (iii. 34, 9).

In several places of the Rig-veda, five classes are generally spoken of such as *pancha-krishtayah*, *pancha-kshitayah*, *pancha-charshanayah*, *pancha-janáh*, *pancha-bhúma*, and *pancha-játá*. There is no clue to be found for the better understanding of what social classifications these classes implied. Mankind, in a collective sense, are said to be distinguished into five classes. Sáyana, following the received tradition of his own time, explains these terms as denoting the four castes with the Nishádas for a fifth. Yáska, in Nirukta (iii. 8), referring to the opinions of older schools, says that these five classes of

* Rig-veda, i. 130, 8; ix. 41, 1.
† Ibid, v. 1, 8, 9; x. 86, 19; i. 103, 3; and vi. 25, 2.

beings are the *Gandharvas, Pitris, Devas, Asuras,* and *Rakshases,* and according to some the four castes, and the barbarian or Nishāda. This meaning seems quite immaterial, and is merely imaginary. When the five classes are designated by so many distinct appellatives, and especially by such a one as *panchabhurah,* it appears that these classifications arose possibly from the different localities the Indo-Aryans first occupied after their advent to India. The authors of the hymns of the *Rig-veda* regarded Manu as the common progenitor of the whole of the Aryan people, either the priests or the chiefs, or those that formed the mass of the population. This notion of descent from one common father overthrows altogether the supposition that the Aryan nation originally consisted of four different castes.

After the population had greatly increased a division of labor became a necessity. The more contemplative among them betook themselves to the worship of the gods, and to the performance of rites and ceremonies at the holy altars; the more powerful class held rule over the rest; and the majority of the population followed various occupations; while the aborigines incorporated themselves in the Indo-Aryan community either as slaves* or as

* *Rig-veda,* viii. 46, 32; Vālkhilya 8, 3.

handicraftsmen. The priesthood was formed only from the employment by the chiefs of individuals known for their rhythmical faculty, knowledge of sacred things, and sanctity, to officiate at the worship of the gods; and the aristocracy formed properly from the class of petty kings. The families of those kings who held sway over single tribes came gradually to occupy a more and more prominent position in the larger kingdoms which were of necessity founded; and thus the military caste was formed. And the people proper, the *vims*, formed a third caste. But the *Sûdras* were a mixed body, partly composed of the aborigines themselves, partly of those Aryans who had settled earlier in India, and partly of those recruits from the later Aryan emigrants who threw off the Brahmanical yoke.

We have however no knowledge of the political condition of the Indo-Aryans, beyond the specification of a number of names of princes. These names are, as might be supposed, peculiar to the Vedas. We have particular intimation, not only of kings, but of envoys and heralds. The kings sent ambassadors to one another; and also employed spies. The political institutions of those days very closely resembled those of the Homeric Greeks. The names for king meant father of the house, and headman of the tribe. Kings are mentioned in the hymns;* and rulers or governors under the titles of pûrapati† and grâmanî‡ are also alluded to. These rulers held powers subject to certain obligations towards a king. The existence of kings, and the mention of taxes, or the contributions from the people for the maintenance of kingdoms imply a settled state of government. Good government is alluded to;§ and the village system also existed during those periods. There were even "halls of justice;" and the complicated law of inheritance was to a certain extent in vogue; and our ancestors had conceptions of the rights of property and definite guarantees for their preservation, knew formalities for transactions of exchange and sale, for payment of wages, and for the administration of oath.

If they were not now strictly agricultural ; they were never a nomadic people. Their chief possessions were the flocks and herds; but by no means they neglected the cultivation of the earth. Fertile water-courses are alluded to ;‖ and the irrigation

---

* Rig-veda, l. 40, 8; i. 126, 1; iii. 43, 5; v. 37, 4; x. 33, 4.
† Ibid, l. 173, 10.
‡ Ibid, x. 62, 11.
§ Ibid, i. 173.
‖ Ibid, iii. 45, 3; x. 43, 7.

of lands under cultivation is also recommended. They measured their fields with a rod. Oxen ploughed their fields; and the articles of food were brought home in carts.

They had domesticated the cow, the sheep, the goat, the horse, and the dog. And the zoology of the *Rig-veda* comprises a great many other animals, such as the lion, tiger, wolf, elephant, camel, deer, ram, bull, serpents, mosquitoes, worms, crocodiles, porpoises, apes, boars, buffaloes, jackals, foxes, rats, and different kinds of birds, i. e. peacocks, pigeons, vultures, ducks, swans, quails, falcons, etc.

The community consisted of the rich and the poor;" and the different occupations pursued were those of priest, poet, physician, barber, carpenter, black-smith, female grinder of corn, carriage builder, worker in wood and metal, manufacturer of weapons of war and other sharpedged implements, boat and ship builder, rope maker, butcher, and the bhisty with his skin brought them water; and grooms rubbed down their horses.

They thought of the means of transit from the earliest times. They had good and great roads and little paths easy to be traversed in mountainous regions and inaccessible places. They navigated

* *Rig-veda*, x. 117.

in oared boats and ferries."* They were a maritime and mercantile nation ; sea-going ships and navigation in the open sea were familiar to them. They were not content with internal trade ; and they undertook sea-voyages as we read of merchants sailing for gain.† Metal money have been in use ; nishkas of gold being mentioned.‡ The use of money in trade may not have been unknown, for "merchants desirous of gain" are cited in the Rik, as sending their ships to the sea.§ We also read of *suvarnas* ; and a *suvarna*, according to Colebrooke, was equal to 16 mâshâs. They were not only familiar with the oceans ; but sometimes must have engaged in naval expeditions. And there is a mention made of a naval expedition under Bhujya, a son of Tugra, against a foreign island, which was only frustrated by a shipwreck.

There were cities (pur) as distinct from villages (grâma).‖ We read of "cities of stone," of "cities

* Rig-veda, I. 97. † Ibid, i. 897.

‡ Ibid, i. 126. According to Manu (vii. 134) a nishka was a weight of gold equal to four suvarnas. Yâska, in his Nirukta, p. 13, quotes from the Vedas, eighteen different words, which convey the abstract idea of wealth, without having any reference to grain, or cattle, or any other object.

§ Rig-veda, i. 48.

‖ Ibid, i. 114, 1; i. 44, 10; i. 149, 4; x. 146, 1.

made of iron,"[*] and of cities with a hundred enclosures or fortifications,[†] which convey the idea of forts consisting of a series of concentric walls. When we read of iron cities we should take them as more substantial than wattle and mud.

They lived in permanent habitations; and their houses were roofed, had windows and doors. Bricks (ishṭakā) were made and known; and lime, mortar, or stucco were used for the purpose of plastering them. The words which occur in the Vedas as the synonymes for houses imply the existence of brick and stone buildings. We read of a house having a thousand doors;[‡] of a palace supported by a thousand columns,[§] of "stately mansion," of "lowly dwelling," of "stone houses," of "carved stones," and of "brick edifices." There were also halls "vast, comprehensive and thousand doored." Vasishṭha longs for a "three storied dwelling;" and Atri is said to have been "thrown into a machine room with a hundred doors where he was roasted."

[*] Rig-veda, i. 58, 8; ii. 20, 8; iv. 27, 1; vii. 3, 7; vii. 15, 14; vii. 95, 1; viii. 89, 8; x. 101, 8.

[†] Ibid, i. 166, 8; vii. 15, 14.

[‡] Ibid, vii. 88, 5.

[§] Ibid, ii. 42, 6.

They lived together with their sons and grandsons; and their domestic economy was founded upon the principles of joint-family system. Their conception of a home approached that of the English—"a pleasant abode,"—"a well dressed wife"—"an irreproachable and beloved wife," "who ornaments the chamber of sacrifice," and "adorns a dwelling," and a "draught of wine." This affectionate domestic character illustrates the happiness of their family life. Although they rejoiced more at the birth of a son, who was in all cases an inheritor of ancestral wealth; yet they showed tender affections for women. The unmarried daughters had a claim upon their father, brother, or other male relatives for subsistence. And even they had claims to a share of the paternal property. Women were active in their occupations; and for them there was needle-work.* The social position of women was considerably higher than it is in modern times. They are spoken of kindly and pleasantly, as "the light of the dwelling." They could converse with their husbands on equal terms, and go together to the sacrifices. They were also quite at liberty to walk and ride abroad; and were, without any reserve, present at public feasts and games. Lovely

* Rig-veda, ii. 282.

maidens appeared in a procession; and grown up unmarried daughters remained without reproach in their father's house. Our ancestors cultivated the laws of morality and civil polity to a great extent. Their social instinct was as old as the religions. The ties of blood were most scrupulously respected; and the extent to which marriage among blood-relations could not be allowed was restricted. The marriage ceremonial was established;* but it is exceedingly difficult to determine in what manner the nuptial ceremonies were performed; and what were the rules observed at such ceremonies. Early marriage was not compulsory and the women enjoyed a freedom of choice in the selection of their husbands.† Remarriage of widows was not prohibited;‡ and a mention is even made of the marriage of a widow with her deceased husband's brother.§ It is to be stated, however, that there is no mention of Śúdras as a class with which Brahmans intermarried. Although intermarriages

* Rig-veda, x. 109.

† Ibid. x. 27, 11, 72; see also Taittiríya-Bráhmana, ii. 4, 2, 7.

‡ Atharva-veda, ix. 5, 27f.; see also Taittiríya-Áranyaka, vi. 1, 1 k.

§ Rig-veda, x. 40, 2.

between these two castes were disapproved, yet we can hardly believe that they were ever prohibited.* Then again polygamy was also tolerated;† though monogamy was the rule.‡ There are also references made to conjugal infidelity.§ Even there were traces of the vices of civilization; for we read in the Vedas of common women, of secret births, of gamblers, and of thieves. Prof. Weber adduces some astounding proofs of the little confidence entertained in ancient times by the Indo-Aryans in the chastity of their women.‖ Notwithstanding all this women were held by the authors of the Bráhmanas in high estimation; but still there are other places in which they are spoken of disparagingly.¶ Adultery was no uncommon occurence.(a) It is also stated that the wife of the person offering *praghásas* to Varuna, must have one or more paramours.(b)

* Vájasaneyí-Samhitá, 23, 30.
† Rig-veda, i. 62, 11; i. 71, 1; i. 105, 8; vii. 26, 3.
‡ Ibid, i. 105, 2; i. 124, 7.
§ Ibid, i. 167, 4; ix. 67, 10ff; x. 34, 4; x. 40, 6.
‖ Nidána-Sútra, iii. 8; see also Satapatha-Bráhmana, iii. 2, 1, 40.
¶ Taittiríya-Samhitá, vi. 5, 8, 2.
(a) Taittiríya-Samhitá, v. 6, 8, 3.
(b) Satapatha-Bráhmana, ii. 5, 2, 20.

Rice, barley, millet, and other kinds of grain, milk, honey, herbs, curd, ripe fruit and clarified butter supplied their usual meal. In the Rig-veda distinct references are made to barley (yava);* and mention of rice (brihi), beans (mâsh), and tila is made in the Atharvan. Parched corn,† cakes (upúpa), and meal prepared with curd or butter are also mentioned.‡ Fruit (phala) is mentioned.§ Bull, ram and buffaloes formed a portion of their food.|| They were also beef eaters.¶ It is true, that there was a time when bovine meat was actually deemed a delightful aliment, a token of generous hospitality in honor of a respected guest or goghna ;(a) and it was even considered an essential accompaniment in the journey from this to the future world; so much so that a cow was in all cases burnt with the dead.

Cooking is described ;(b) and in preparing flesh meat, part was boiled in a caldron, part was roasted

* Rig-veda, I. 23, 15 ; i. 66, 3 ; i. 117, 21 etc.
† Ibid, I. 16, 2 ; iii, 35, 3 ; iii. 52, 5 ; vi. 29, 4.
‡ Ibid, iii. 52, 7 ; vi. 57, 2.
§ Ibid, iii. 45, 4.
|| Ibid, i. 164, 13 ; v. 29, 7 ; viii. 12, 8 ; viii. 66, 10 ; x. 27. 17.
¶ Wilson's Rig-veda, I. p. 165 ; iii. pp. 103, 276, 410 & 453.
(a) Asiatic Researches, vii. p. 288. (b) Rig-veda, ii. 117.

on spits, and part was made into balls. There were vessels to distribute the broth; dishes with covers, and skewers and knives. The queens and wives assisted in cooking and preparing the every day meal and the banquet. There were different kinds of earthen cooking pots (kapálas). We read of kalasa or jar; and of kilns or furnaces for the baking of such vessels. And frequent mention is made of "potters," and of "potter's wheel." The material which was used in the manufacture of domestic vessels was not only clay, but also wood and leather, and even metals. They had "golden cups," plates of gold, silver, bronze, and magnetic iron; leather skins for water, and leather bottles.

Wine was in use.* Swillers of wine are mentioned.† Our ancestors were much addicted to the drinking of spirits; and indulged excessively both in soma and other strong drinks. Wine or spirit was in a public manner sold in shops solely opened with this view, for the general use of the community. In the Rig-veda a hymn occurs which shows beyond all controversy that wine was kept in leather bottles,‡ and sold without any reserve to all comers. The

---

* Rig-veda, i. 116, 7; vii. 86, 6; x. 107, 9.
† Ibid, viii. 21, 14.
‡ Wilson's Rig-veda, ii. p. 204.

Taittirīya-Brāhmaṇa contains mantras from which we learn about the preparation of the liquor; but no information is available as to how the distillation was effected.

Our ancestors made considerable progress in their dress. But no information is available regarding the form and shape of it. It is possible that the mass of the population wore scarfs or plaidlike articles. The Rig-veda contains many texts which show that they were perfectly familiar with the art of weaving. We read of "a woman weaving a garment," of "female weavers," of the "warp and the woof," of "putting on becoming attire," of "a well attired female," of "a well dressed woman," of "elegant garments," and of also "elegant well-made garments" as fit for honorary presents. In the Yajur and Sāma Vedas there are many allusions made to clothing; and in the former even "gold cloth" or "brocade" is mentioned.* Furs, skins, cotton, and wool were the only materials of which clothing was made; and even various colors were used in dyeing textile fabrics. Silk is nowhere mentioned; but Pāṇini has it.† Mention of the needle and sewing has been met with; and there can be no doubt that

* Taittirīya-Brāhmaṇa, iii. 675.
† सिद्धान्त | 4, 3, 42.

our ancestors were familiar with dresses made with the aid of scissors* and needle. They wore turbans; and turban under the name of *ushnisha* appears in the Atharva-veda (xv. 2, 1).† Female modesty required also covering of the body down to the ankles; and the breasts were never to be exposed. Women always wore a sheet and kánchuka over their body clothes; and moved about with shoes or pattens on.‡

The Indo-Aryans, as a rule, never cultivated the beard; and even in those early times razor and barber were in every day requisition.§ Allusions to shaving are made.‖ Boots, shoes and pattens were also in fashion in those days. The material of which these were made was bovine leather. Pániní gives words for boots; and, according to Súmvatya as cited by A'svaláyana, the hide of the sacrificial cattle was even used as material for shoes, and for other household articles. They had umbrellas also.¶ They had fondness for ornaments and for decoration of the different parts of the body. We read of "golden ornaments," of "golden collars," "bracelets," and

* Rig-veda, viii. 4, 16.
† Muir's Sanskrit Texts, v. 462.
‡ Bühler's A'pastamba, p. 14.
§ Wilson's Rig-veda, iv. p. 293.
‖ Rig-veda, x. 142, 4.
¶ Ibid. vi. 4, 97.

"fingerrings," of "an adorable uniform necklace," of "golden earings," "anklets and tiaras," and of "jewel necklaces." In the Brâhmana of the Yajur-veda jewellery is said to be strung in gold.* Whether looking glasses formed part of the toilet is very doubtful. They had musical instruments of shells and reeds; and there is mention made of a harp with a hundred strings. Dancers afforded them entertainment;† and for their amusement they had also puppets and stage exhibitions.‡

They had carriages and war chariots drawn by horses; and bullock carts and wagons. The carriages were made of wood and mounted on brazen wheels; and had iron reins and pillars. Those carriages had seats§ and awnings;‖ and they were "easy going," and sometime "inlaid with gold." There were chariots, spacious and richly ornamented with three metals gold, silver and copper; and fitted with golden trappings. We also read of "three columned triangular car," of "golden three shafted chariots," of "golden wheels covered with iron weapons," and of "arming the wheels." In the *Rig*-veda "three

* Taittirîya-Brâhmana, iii. 669.
† *Rig*-veda, i. 92, 4.
‡ Ibid. iii. 195.
§ Ibid. i. 175.
‖ Ibid. i. 94.

benches as fixtures in each car, and the space sufficient for several persons and some goods" are repeatedly mentioned. They had also whips.

Gold, silver, copper and iron were known and worked. And they appear to have been the first to discover how to turn iron into steel. They used golden mail or raiment,* the "coat of mail," "golden breast-plates," "cuirasses of leather," "cotton-quilted cuirass," "iron mail and armour." The Rig-veda notices banners; and the war cry is also alluded to. The drum† was the instrument for marshalling troops or giving orders to them. The martial wind instrument is also mentioned.‡ The army consisted of both foot soldiers and mounted troops. We read of arrows having feathery wings, the horns of the deer forming their points. But arrows were generally made of the sara reed usually with a blade of iron, and besmeared with poison. Their weapons and other implements were swords, spears, lances, helmets, javelins, war missiles, discus, clubs, bucklers, bows, quivers, arrows, shafts, axes, razor, scissors, knives, hatchets, and hooks; and those that were of metal were sharpened on grindstones.

* Rig-veda, i. 25, 10, 13.
† Ibid, i. 28, 5; vi. 47, 29, 31.
‡ Ibid, i. 117, 21.

Religion moulded Indian life, and all its social and political institutions; and even to it is ascribable the origin of investigations in all the departments of knowledge. Astronomical observations were first carried on simply with a view to fix the right time for the performance of the sacrifices; and the earliest beginnings of geometrical and mathematical investigations among them arose also from certain sacrificial requirements. The laws of phonetics were cultivated because it would have been a grave offence to the gods to pronounce wrongly a single letter of the sacrificial formulas; grammar and etymology were likewise studied simply for the right understanding of the holy scriptures. And philosophy and theology have ever been closely connected.

They counted beyond a hundred.* The Sulvasûtras of Baudhâyana and of Âpastamba, and the Sulvaparisishta of Kâtyâyana contain a number of interesting rules for the construction of the various altars, which could not be done without some amount of geometrical knowledge. The property of the right-angled triangle was known to them. They also tried to express the relation between the diagonal and the side of a square, and arrived at a very close approximation. But the most interesting

* White Yajur-veda, xvii.

attempt they made in the cultivation of geometrical operations was that of squaring the circle.

The mention of the "star-gazers," of the "calculator," of "observers of the stars," and "the science of astronomy," warrants us to conclude that astronomical science was then actively cultivated. The quinquennial circle was known to them; and the division of the year was made into twelve (or 13, i. e., the intercalary month*) months consisting of 360 days, and each day having 30 muhúrtas. The moon was the measurer of time; and there is apparently an expression of an astronomical fact that she shines only through reflecting the light of the sun. They knew that "the sun does never set nor rise."† A close observation of the moon's progress, and of the appearance of the group of stars near which she passed, was already made. They had also the conception of the use of the lunar and solar years; and of the method of adjusting the one to the other.‡ And they determined the cardinal points of the horizon, and calculated the eclipses.§ It is an interesting fact that even they had some knowledge

---

* Rig-veda, i. 2.
† Haug's Aitareya-Bráhmana, ii. p. 242.
‡ Rig-veda, i. 25.
§ Ibid. iv. 2. 12.

of the laws of attraction;[a] and it is not improbable that the law of gravitation may have been one of those known to them.

We read of the constellations;[*] and the zodiac comprises a division of the circle of the heavens into 27 equal portions, each consisting of 13 and ⅓ degrees. It is to be understood that this division could not have been made without an instrument. Our ancestors must have possessed a knowledge of the use of appropriate apparatus like the armillary sphere to explain the lunar zodiac, and to illustrate its use. The division of the heavens into twenty-seven Nakshatras, a division which is the soul of the sacred calendar, and according to which all the Vaidik sacrifices were performed, is said not to have been indigenous to India, but borrowed from without. M. Biot published several articles in the Journal des Savans, in which he essayed to prove the Chinese origin of the Indian Nakshatras. He maintained that the number of the Nakshatras was originally 28, and afterwards reduced to 27. There occurs one allusion to these Nakshatras in the Veda;[†] and the 27 divisions with their asterisms and presiding deities

* Rig-veda. ix. 80-12.
† Ibid. i. 50.
‡ Ibid, x. 85, 2.

are spoken of in the Bráhmanas. But notwithstanding these facts it has been urged that the division of the heavens into 27 was borrowed from China. The originality of the Vedas is certainly destroyed, in case it is proved that even at that early age a foreign civilization exercised influence upon the growth of the Indian mind. M. Biot supported his favorite propositions with so much learning and skill that so ingenious a scholar as Prof. Lassen took his side, and admitted the introduction of the Chinese *Sieu* into northern India before the 14th century B. C.* According to M. Biot's own statements the number of the Chinese *Sieu* was only 24, and was not raised to 28 till the year 1100 B. C. Astronomy, at least that portion of it, which bears relation to the Nakshatras, or the twenty-seven lunar mansions of the Indo-Aryans, is closely connected with the Vaidik worship.

Vaidik sacrifices could not have been in any case performed without a knowledge of the lunar mansions. The Indian names of the months were derived from the names of the constellations; and the names of the constellations again were derived, for the most part, from the names of ancient Vaidik deities.†

* Indian Antiquities, p. 747.
† Whitney's Súrya-Siddhánta, p. 203.

The exact time of the lunar festivals is fixed with such close accuracy, that the Indo-Aryans, at the time when those public sacrifices gained ground, must have been, in a high degree, proficient in astronomy. The growth of astronomical knowledge in India, is closely connected with the intellectual and especially the religious history of that country. The original division of the year into lunar months must have taken effect prior to the first separation of the great Aryan family. If we find the same names of the months in Sanskrit and Chinese; and if these names the Chinese Dictionary cannot explain, surely the conclusion must be that they were borrowed by the Chinese from the Indo-Aryans, and not by the Indo-Aryans from the Chinese. The three winter months are designated in Chinese as Pehoua, Mokoé, and Phalkana; and these names correspond with the three Indian months Pausha, Mâgha, and Phâlguna. These Indian months received their names from the corresponding Nakshatras Pushyâ, Maghâ, and Phâlgunî. Shall we infer, then, that the Indo-Aryans borrowed the idea of the lunar Nakshatras from the Chinese, or that the Chinese borrowed them from the Indo-Aryans? The Nakshatras were indeed suggested to the Indo-Aryans by the moon's sideral revolution; and their number was originally 27 and not

28. The *Sien* were originally 24 in number, and they were afterwards raised to 28. It must be observed here that there is no trace to be found of a like change in India. The *manâzil* of the Arabians were also directly derived from India. The Chinese system of *Sien* differs from the Indian system of Nakshatras both in its structure and its object. The object of the Nakshatra system was to mark the progress of the sun, moon, and planets through the heavens. This Nakshatra system had from the beginning a strictly scientific structure and application. The relation of the Chinese *Sien* to the Nakshatras, is altogether out of the question. The *Sien* throughout are but single stars;* while the *Târâs* are clusters of stars. The attempt to identify the Chinese *Sien* with the Indian Nakshatras, or 27 lunar mansions, is decidedly futile.

Another sign of social progress we gain from their knowledge of herbs and mode of medical treatment. "Ambrosia," says a son of Kanva, "is in the waters." "All medicaments are in the waters," thus anticipating in so remote antiquity the hydropathic doctrine of the present century. They had the knowledge of the three humours of the body, i. e., wind, bile, and phlegm; and of the hygenic

* Whitney's Sûrya-Siddhânta, p. 207.

properties of water, air, and vegetables. Agni is said to be the remover of deseases; and the Asvins are called physicians of the gods, and they are said to have given sight to Kanvn.* Soma is also supposed to preside over medicinal herbs. Anatomical observations were then simply made by dissecting the victims at the sacrifices. At any rate animal anatomy was perfectly understood, as each of the different parts of the body had its own well defined name. There is ample evidence of the practice of medicine in those early days when we read of the "doctor who seeks a patient."

* Rig-veda, i. 117.

CHAPTER III.

Vaidik Theogony and Mythology—Abstract Conceptions of the Deity—Cosmogony—Vaidik Doctrine of a Future Life—Priesthood and Vaidik Ceremonials of Worship.

There is a faculty of faith in man, a power independent of sense and reason which is the primordial source of any religion, which enables him to apprehend the Infinite. In the hymns we hear in unmistakable language the lispings of infancy, the yearnings of struggling spirits for something that is neither conceivable or utterable. And even in such mental struggles they, as the case may be, differed in their conception of the deity; and they made no distinction between the concrete and the abstract, nor between the material and the spiritual. In the first stage of thought when the mind had not risen to the conception of the unity of God as the sole Creator and Governor of all things, it is but natural that the bright objects of nature should draw the human breast; and thus the sun, moon and other objects would be worshipped and adored as they appeared to be of an unbounded power; and that the different domains of nature should be allotted to different gods, each of whom presiding over his own province. But in the Rigveda even such departments are not clearly defined, and we thus see that one domain was presided over by more than one deity. Thunder, lightning, rain, mists, and hail filled the desponding mind of our ancestors with terror. When the mind of man so simple and childlike begins to reflect upon the powerful and unintelligible forces of nature, it perceives its own weakness, and offers sacrifices to them. It moreover represents them sometimes as benevolent, and sometimes as terrible, ascribing to them the very same character which must be the result of the association of their daily life. The birth of certain gods is even conceived; and such birth has no other than a physical meaning. But the general absence of anthropomorphism from the Vaidik notions of divine beings is conspicuous." The origin of almost all mythological legends is solely attributable to the ascribing of human agency to other beings and even to animate things, and consequently to their

a "The Vedas hold out precautions against framing a Deity after human imagination, and recommend mankind to direct all researches towards the surrounding objects, viewed, either collectively or individually, bearing in mind their regular, wise, and wonderful combinations and arrangements."—Introduction to the Abridgment of the Vedanta by Raja Rammohun Roy, p. vii.

ultimate personification. However it was simply the first stage in the growth of Vaidik mythology; but language has never been at rest to spin it. It has been very appropriately said that mythology was the bane of the ancient world, a desease of language. It is nevertheless history changed into fable, which is full of interesting problems that supply ample materials for the history of Aryan thought. And it is also most valuable to the student of history not only in a philological, but also a philosophical, and more especially a psychological point of view.

Yâska, following the ancient expounders who preceded him, has reduced the gods to three, viz., Agni whose place is on the earth; Vâyu, or Indra, whose place is in the atmosphere; and Sûrya whose place is in the sky.* Besides this triple classification the gods are sometimes said to be thirty-three in number;† and sometimes as being much more numerous, i.e., three hundred, three thousand, thirty and nine.‡ They again are divided into great and small, young and old;§ and though frequently described as

---

* Nirukta, vii. 5., and compare Rig-veda, x. 158, 1.

† Rig-veda, i. 34, 11; i. 45, 2; I. 139, 11; viii. 28, 1; viii. 30, 2; viii. 35, 3; ix. 92, 4; and compare Satapatha-Brâhmaṇa, iv. 5, 7, 2.

‡ Rig-veda, iii. 39. § Rig-veda, I. 27, 13.

immortal,† they are in no manner spoken of as self-existing beings, and without beginning.

Dyaus and Prithivi are invoked to attend religious rites, and to grant various boons. They are characterized as possessing both the physical characteristics, and moral and spiritual nature. They are jointly called parents; but elsewhere the Heaven is singly called father and the Earth mother. They are not only the parents of men but of the gods also. They are said to be the creator and sustainer of all things; but passages are not wholly wanting where they are spoken of as themselves created. Though Indra is said to be their creator, they are spoken of as also created by Soma, Pûshan, Dhâtri, and Hiranyagarbha. Even they are said to have received their shape from Tvashtri, and to have sprung from the head and the feet of Purusha; and to be supported by Mitra, Savitri, Varuna, Indra, Agni, Soma and Hiranyagarbha.

Aditi is the only goddess spoken of by name in the *Rig*-veda. She is styled the goddess or the divine, and is the source and supporter of all things, and represents the whole of nature. She is supplicated for different blessings, and for forgiveness

† *Rig*-veda, l. 24, 1; i. 72, 2, 10; l. 180, 3; iii. 21, 1; iv. 42, 1; x. 13, 1; x. 60, 9.

of sins. She is said to be the mother of Varuna and of other gods; and her gifts are pure and celestial. She, as the great power, wields the forces of the universe, and controls men by moral laws. In the Sáma-veda Aditi is represented with her sons and brothers. The sons are styled A'dityas, and they are Mitra, Aryaman, Bhaga, Varuna, Daksha, and Ansa.* But in some places they are stated to be seven, in others eight in number, though their names are not given there. They are described as sleepless, many-eyed, vast, strong, bright, holy, pure, golden, sinless, blameless. They are far-observing; and all things are near to them. They see the good and evil in men's hearts, and punish sin.

Mitra is frequently associated with Varuna. Varuna, however, is sometimes separately celebrated; Mitra but seldom. Mitra seems to be more connected with the day, and Varuna with the night. Mitra and Varuna are the most important from the identification of the former with the Mithra of the Zendavesta;† and of the latter with the Ouranos of the

* Rig-veda, ii. 27, 1.

† Herodotus confounds Mitra with Mylitta: but the important thing to observe is, that Mitra was a Persian god. But there are evidently many passages in the Vandidâd which prove that among the ancient Persians Mithra was sometimes

Greeks. Varuna occupies a rather more prominent place in the hymns; he presides over the light, and it is said in one passage that the constellations are his holy acts, and that the moon moves by his command. He is called the source of light: he grants wealth, averts evil, and protects cattle. In another passage, he is said to abide in the ocean, and to be acquainted with the course of ships. He is also said to know the flight of birds in the sky, and the periodical succession of the months. His character does not, however, appear to have been the same throughout the whole period represented by the Vaidik hymns. He is the sovereign of his own abode, and a king both of gods and men often surrounded by his messengers. He is mighty, fixed in purpose, far-sighted and visible to his worshippers. To him are attributed the grandest cosmical functions. He is said to have created heaven and earth; and to uphold, and rule over them. He possesses high moral character more than any other gods. His laws are fixed and unimpeachable, and he controls over the destinies of men. He is besought to drive away evil, give deliverance from sin, and prolong life. The same attributes and functions are also ascribed

represented as the Sun. The modern Pársis understand by it Meher Izad, in contradistinction to Khurshíd, the Sun.

to Mitra. Varuna however was an older god than Indra; and the homage originally paid to the former was gradually transferred to the latter. That Varuna worship declined, and Indra worship superseded it, was the result of the gradual change which marked the Indo-Aryan religion. The anteriority of Varuna to Indra is borne out by the coincidence of his name with the Ouranos of the Greek mythology; while all attempt at the identification of Indra with any other character of the same mythology is out of the question.

Indra was human; he is reputed as the destroyer of Vritra, an Asura or Assyrian. And for his exploits he was at last deified. He is described as being born, and as having both the parents. He is also said to have been produced by the gods; and to have sprung from the mouth of Purusha. He is a twin brother of Agni. The highest divine attributes and functions are attributed to him. He is spoken of in some places as having physical superiority, and in others as having no spiritual elevation or moral grandeur; though there are various other texts in which he is found to be invested with ethical character. He is besought by men like a father, and for temporal blessings; and even faith in him is enjoined. He is represented to be heroic, strong, martial, ancient, youthful, undecaying and wielder of thunderbolt. He is golden, and can assume any shape at will. His wife is alluded to; and his intimate relation with his worshippers is spoken of. He is the destroyer of enemies; and he conquered heaven by austerity.

Vâyu is frequently found in conjunction with Indra, and does not seem to occupy a very prominent place in the Rig-veda. He is the son-in-law of Tvashtri, and is spoken of as beautiful, and handsome in form. Pûshan is the protector on a journey, particularly of robbers: he is said to be the divinity presiding over the earth. The character of Rudra is similar; but he is the source of fertility, and giver of happiness; and he evidently presides over medicinal plants, and is invoked for the removal of diseases. He is represented as the lord of evil spirits. He was originally an object of worship with the aborigines; and such worship was gradually adopted by the Indo-Aryans. The Maruts, or Rudras are the sons of Rudra and Prisni. They are very commonly represented as the attendants of Indra, and as children of the ocean. They are spoken of as golden-footed; and they worship Indra. The invocations of the Visvedevâs as they are called, represent a later phase of thought than the invocations of each individual deity singly.

Agni (the name is identical with the Latin Ignis) is indeed called the lowest of the gods, but notwithstanding this he is greatly revered. He is invoked at all the sacrifices; and as the sacrificial fire, he is the servant of both men and gods, carrying the invocations and the offerings of the former to the latter; he invites the gods to the ceremonies; and performs them in behalf of the lord of the house. Represented as a divinity, his is immortality, his is never-failing youth, invested with infinite power and glory. He is the granter of life, health, food, wealth and caitle. He is the source of effulgent light, and the destroyer of all things. He is golden-haired, and an emblem of purity. He is known under various appellations; and many deities inferior to him are purely his manifestations. He is identified with Vishnu, Varuna, Mitra, Indra, Aryaman, Amsa, Tvashtri, Rudra, Púshan, Savitri, Bhaga, Aditi, Hotrá, Bháratí, Iá, Sarasvatí; and the functions and attributes of other deities are often ascribed to him. He is the son of heaven and earth; and elsewhere he is said to have been generated by the gods, and to have been brought from the sky by Mátarisvan. His production is also attributed to the waters. He again is the father of the gods, and is regarded as having a triple existence. He knows the races of gods and men. He is the protector, friend and leader of the people. He is the divine king, and is as strong as Indra, and is worshipped by by Varuna, Mitra, the Maruts, and all the three thousand, three hundred and thirty-nine gods.

Sûrya, or the Greek ἥλιος, and Savitri, are exact personifications of the sun; and under these two different epithets the sun is chiefly represented in the hymns. Sûrya is spoken of as an Âditya, and occupies a place in Vaidik worship not so prominent as could be naturally anticipated from the magnificence and splendour of that luminous body. He is said to be god-born, and to have been generated by Indra, Agni, Soma, Mitra, and Varuna. He is the divine leader or priest of the gods. Like Agni and Indra, he is the source of light, and the granter of temporal blessings. He is all-seeing, and beholds the good and bad deeds of mortals. He is said to be the healer of leprosy. Only three súktas in the first book of the Rig-veda are addressed to him; and these "convey no very strikingly expressive acknowledgment of his supremacy." Although sun-worship was not prominent, the Indo-Aryans loved light and even warmth, and the sun, the "ray diffuser." The expressions contained in the hymns relating to this deity exhibit a careful and loving observation of Nature. He is spoken of as coming "from a distance," and "removing all sins;" or as the divine Sun he is supplicated to take away the "sickness of the heart," and the "yellowness of the body."

Savitri is sometimes distinguished from Sûrya; and is frequently identified with Mitra and Pûshan. He is the golden deity, yellow-haired, golden-handed, and golden-tongued. He is the bestower of all desirable things; and confers blessings from the sky, from the atmosphere, and from the earth. He is said to have bestowed immortality on the gods.

The Asvins are in various texts connected with Sûrya. They are the twin sons of Vivasvat and Saranyû; and are also called the sons of the sky. They are described as young, beautiful, ancient, strong, bright, terrible, and skilful. They bestow food and wealth. They ever occupy themselves with multifarious earthly transactions, enable the worshippers to baffle their enemies, assist them in their need, and extricate them from difficulty. Their business is more earthly than heavenly. They cure the blind, the lame, the emaciated, and the sick. They are besought for different blessings; for long life, offspring, wealth, victory, destruction of enemies, and forgiveness of sins. The myth of the human Asvins has two distinct elements, one cosmical and the other human or historical; which have in course of time become blended into one. The cosmical element refers to their luminous nature; and the human element to the wonderful cures effected by them. They might have been some renowned mortals, horsemen of celebrity, who were admitted on account of their wonderful medical skill to the companionship of the gods.

Trashtri is frequently found connected with Ribhus. He is the divine artisan; and is also versed in all magical devices. He forges the thunderbolts of Indra. He is the skilful worker, and the creator of all forms. He bestows long life, offspring, wealth and protection; and forms husband and wife. He is supplicated to preserve the worshippers. He was also a renowned mortal; and as the skilful artisan he had been translated into the companionship of the gods.

Soma is the god who plays an important part in the sacrificial act of the Vaidik age. He is said to be divine, and the soul of sacrifice. He is the king of gods and men. He is the lord of creatures, and the generator of the sky, earth, of Agni,

Sûrya, Indra, and Vishṇu. He is wise, strong, agile, and thousand-eyed. He beholds all worlds, and destroys the irreligious. He is immortal, and confers immortality on gods and men. He is generous as a father to a son; and is supplicated to forgive sins. In the post-Vaidik age the name Soma came to be commonly applied to the moon and its regent. Even in the Rig-veda some traces of this application seem to be discoverable.*

The connexion of the personified Dawn or Ushas with Sûrya makes its worship a form of solar adoration. The language of the hymns addressed to her, involves no mystery. The invigorating influence which the dawn exercises on both body and mind, and the luminous and other pleasant phenomena connected with day-break, constitute the subject of some of the best portions of Vaidik poetry; and out of them the conceptions of Ushas arise. She is invoked as the affluent, as the giver of food, and bringer of opulence; she is asked to lavish on the pious riches, horses, cattle, posterity, and troops

* x. 85, 3 and 5; and compare "The transference of the name Soma to the moon, which appears in the later history of the Indian religion, is hitherto obscure: the Vedas do not know it, nor do they seem to prepare the way for it in any manner." Journal of the American Oriental Society, iii. p. 309.

of slaves; and she is praised for the numerous and various boons she has bestowed on the worshippers who were liberal to her. She is the goddess imbued with an excellent intellect, truthful, and fulfiller of her promises. She invigorates the diligent; when she appears, bipeds and quadrupeds "are in motion;" the winged birds hover in the air; and men who have to earn their bread quit their homes. She rides, in a golden chariot, which is large and beautiful. The relation of Ushas to other Vaidik deities is two-fold, physical and ritual, in as much as the phenomena of the dawn are associated with the other phenomena of Nature, and as certain religious ceremonies are held at the beginning of the day. For this, she is frequently addressed as the daughter of heaven; and when her parents are spoken of, the commentator explains this word as signifying heaven and earth. She is further called the daughter of the night; but, on other grounds, she is also described as having Night for her sister. She is, besides, the sister of Bhaga and Varuna; and the faithful wife of Sûrya.

Sarasvati is a goddess of some importance in the *Rig-veda*. She is celebrated both as a river and as a deity. She of course was primarily a river deity. She bestows prosperity, wealth, offspring, and fertility. She attends the sacrifices along with other goddesses, Bhárati, Hotrá, Varútri, Mahi, Ilá, Dhishaná. Aranyáni is mentioned as the goddess of forest solitude. Rákā, Sinivāli, and Gungū, are three other goddesses represented in the hymns. Rákā is closely connected with parturition. Sraddhā is an object of adoration in the morning, at noon, and at sunset. She is the personification of an abstract idea or religious faith. She prospers the liberal worshippers of the gods, and imparts faith. Lakshmi and Sri do not occur in the hymns in the sense as they appear in the later mythology. Sri is mentioned as issuing forth from Prajápati when he was wrapped up in intense austerity. Aditi, the mother of the Ádityas, is the representative of the universe; Diti her counterpart, Nishtigri is the mother, and Indráni, the wife of Indra. Prisni is the mother of the Maruts. Súryā is the daughter of the sun, and the spouse of the Asvins, or of Soma. These goddesses and few others, such as Agnáyí, Varunání, Rodasi are also celebrated in the hymns of the Rig-veda.

The gods are merely poetical names; which gradually assumed a divine personality never thought of by the original authors. Names after names were created to express the infinity and majesty of the divine; and this could only have been suggested by the consciousness of the insufficiency of those names that had been already formed and used with the same view. The common names of the deities had originally their material meaning; but gradually they came to be used in the spiritual sense. Every name was created with a distinct purpose; and so had a history full of meaning. And even an idea of a deity under such varying disguises evinces a great progress of thought. The names are sometimes used merely as appellatives; and sometimes as names of gods. It is, however, clear that many names were created in the state of utter helplessness to express the ideas of the deity. As could be the various conceptions of the different poets, so the natures of the gods must have differentiated. The same god is said in one hymn to be as supreme and equal; and again in another as inferior to others. However the whole nature of these ideal and imaginary gods is still transparent; they are merely names of natural phenomena and without being; they are the creations of man and not his creators. Here names play with us. But the consciousness that all the deities are but different names of one and the same godhead is manifest in many of the hymns of the Veda. In one hymn it is distinctly stated that the gods, though differently named and represented, are really one and the same; but men only call them by different names, and the poets express the same god in different forms:—"They call him Indra, Mitra, Varuna, Agni; and (he is) the celestial Garutmat. Sages name variously that which is but one:—they call it Agni, Yama, Mâtarisvan."* And as regards the character and functions of Tvashtri we have an approach to the idea of a supreme creator of the universe. According to the Taittiriya-Brâhmana the gods attained their divine rank by austerity.† They are said to possess the qualities of Rishis. This possibly implies that the Rishis thought to possess particular knowledge of the deities, with whom they again believed that they had affinity. "Indeed, the relations between the Vaidik Aryans and their deities appear to have been of a childlike and filial character; the evils which they suffered, they ascribed to some offence of omission or commission which had been given to a deity; whilst the good which they received was

* Rig-veda, i. 164, 46.
† Muir's Original Sanskrit Texts, iii. p. 275.

in like manner ascribed to his kindness and favor."* The highest deities of the primitive Aryan times represented not only the conspicuous processes of external nature; but also the higher relations of moral and social life. The songs with which the Indo-Aryans invoked the gods clearly show that they sought them for their spiritual as well as for their material welfare. Ethical considerations are not, therefore, extraneous to these instinctive outbursts of the pious mind. Sin and evil, indeed, are often adverted to; and the gods are extolled because they destroy sinners and evil-doers. However, there are to be found many hymns in the Rik which depart materially from the simplicity of the conception here alluded to.

Our Aryan ancestors carried with them their religion when they started from their primitive home, and spread over the various parts of the world. Therefore, among different branches of the family there is to be found a great harmony in their original worship, and in the names of God and the gods. Indeed the Indo-Aryans, Greeks, Romans, Germans, Celtics at one time worshipped the same gods. Although the Indo-Aryan mythology is extravagant

* Wheeler's History of India, I. p. 13.

and ridiculous, and has an icy coldness of meaning in it, yet those mythological dreams have an enduring symbolic value, and stand as data of pristine history. The Indo-Aryans early speculated largely on matters supernatural; and their religion was an important feature of their civilization. The Vaidik religion is the true expression of the view which our simple-minded but highly gifted ancestors imbued with deep religious feelings, took of the wonderful powers and phenomena of nature. And it originated in the whole body of the people, and not in the minds of single individuals, whether inspired or not inspired. In the hymns there is a deep awakening of the religious sentiment, and a sense of the divine. In all the objects of nature our ancestors beheld either the primary causes of them, or the visible emblems of the invisible great cause. But once the religious faculty is roused, the human mind which is subtle, introversive and contemplative, could never be satisfied with the mere idea that the elements are the sole causes of creation; and so it must go on to spiritualize the gigantic forms of nature by which we are surrounded, and as to the extent to which the beautiful conceptions of poetic fancy are carried, religion must of necessity become fetchism, pantheism, or polytheism. And polytheism can only be the result when each spirit is allowed to assume a separate form, and is invested with attributes as worthy as could be of its emblem. In the oldest portions of the hymns, there are few traces to be found of abstract conceptions of the deity. They apparently disclose the primitive stage of religious belief of simple men who, under the influence of the most wonderful phenomena of nature, felt every where the presence and agency of divine powers; and who then had not risen to a clear idea of one Supreme God. Our ancestors imagined that each of the provinces of the universe was controlled by each of the deities; and this is clearly shown by the special functions assigned to them, and by the very names which they hold.

The Vedas contain no real system; they never classify nor define the objects of worship. This was, however, done at last by commentators, who seem to have generally misunderstood the religion taught in them. There are numerous passages in the Rig-veda in many of which a monotheistic and in many others a pantheistic tendency is very clearly manifested. In the later stage of reflection our ancestors very possibly made approximations to monotheistic tendencies; and those approximations could only be weak and sporadic; and that such a speculative monotheism was of necessity of a barren and shadowy character. In the hymns there are traces of human conceptions, human aspirations, human wisdom, and human folly. They have their material and spiritual aspect; they are at once vaguely pantheistic, severely monotheistic, grossly polytheistic, and coldly atheistic. They contain but the common principle of all the four. This prehistoric star-dust of all the systems may properly be called pantheism not in exclusive sense. It is not philosophical abstraction but intense realisation. The polytheism of the Vedas like their pantheism is in the free, plastic age. The complicated polytheism which we find in the hymns is but the full development of polytheism of anterior centuries. It is evident that monotheism was never the starting point of the Vaidik system. We cannot conceive at the first stage of thought of the unity existing under the diversity; and such a conception as the first fruit of theosophic philosophy, is decidedly of later growth, and the result of subsequent reflection and comparision. We are therefore to believe that monotheism never preceded polytheism. When the human spirit is once gifted with clear intuitions to conceive of the unity of nature and its Author, it is not possible that it would ignore that original cognition, and betake itself to the vagaries of naturalism and the worship of the multifarious deities of the proper Vaidik Olympus.

The ideas of entity and non-entity were very well familiar to the Vaidik Rishis.* In the 90th hymn of the tenth book of the Rig-veda the unity of the godhead is recognised, although in a clearly pantheistic sense. We see elsewhere that the sun, the sky, and the earth were at one time considered as natural objects, generated by the gods; and at another time as themselves the gods who created all things. Some scholars have gone so far as to assert that the idea of one God breaks through the mist of a polytheistic and an idolatrous phraseology. This is a mistake. The human mind in its natural operation strives to reduce all objects and events of knowledge to unity and harmony, and to trace everything to a single source; and until there could be made a sufficient progress towards the knowledge of the unity and harmony of this marvellous universe, it is not possible for men to attain to a real conception of the unity of the godhead.

* Rig-veda, x. 72.

Oneness of God does not however exclude the idea of plurality of gods. There was no word yet to express the abstract idea of an immaterial and supernatural Being. The attributes of supremacy and omnipotence ascribed to one god did by no means exclude the admission of the gods or names of gods. And it is also clear from the hymns that the poets never thought of other gods when they addressed their own god. The Vaidik hymns are both physiolatrous and polytheistic. The age when they were composed, as appears clearly from the Bráhmaṇas or directories for their use in the Brahma sacrifices, was followed by a palpable deterioration in the thought and feeling of the Indo-Aryans. At first the polytheism was simple. "The polytheistic idea, however, when once it had begun to work, would tend constantly to multiply the number of divinities, as we see it has already done in the Vaidik age."* There never was nor could be a pure polytheism or a pure monotheism. It is beyond doubt, that the human mind, as in the degree it observes and reflects, advances more rapidly towards monotheism. But it is to be confessed that such movement is very slow, and often

* Pictet's Origines Indo-Européennes, ii. pp. 708 ff.

obstructed by tradition and habit. We must not place at the commencement that which ought to be placed at the very end. However it is clear and fully admitted that our ancestors were polytheists before their separation; and they could never completely forget what they once learnt and brought with them as a heritage from their original home. Such teaching, which again they had left as a legacy, had acted most forcibly on the mind of their descendants from generations to generations, until the proper philosophical age dawned, and the Upanishads were composed and their doctrines had taken ground. But the influence of such philosophical writings has been in no way complete nor permanent; and their attempts towards obliteration at once from the mind, of the polytheistic principles, were far from being successful.

The Indo-Aryans had not attained to a clear and logical comprehension of the characteristics which they themselves ascribed to the objects of their worship. The conceptions of the godhead indicated in the hymns are of a fluctuating and undecided character. The remarkable representations of a host of subordinate objects of worship, exhibit to us a conception of the universe by our ancestors which was mythical, sacramental, polytheistic, and even pantheistic. In the childhood of the world, the Indo-Aryans possessing simple and reflective minds solved the mysterious and difficult problem of the production of the existing universe in various ways. They entertained a great number of different conjectures with regard to cosmogony. As the case may be, they ascribed it sometimes to physical, and sometimes to spiritual powers. And as speculation gradually acquired vigour, different opinions asserted themselves, and they in like manner became perplexed; and one of them asks "What was the forest, what was the tree, out of which they fashioned heaven and earth? Enquire with your minds, ye sages, what was that on which he (Visvakarman) took his stand when supporting the world?"* Another poet asks, "Which of these two was the first, and which the last? How have they been produced? Sages, who knows?"† And as further speculations were carried on they gradually arrived at the idea of the universe having sprung out of darkness and a pre-existing chaos‡ this notion could only have presented

* Rig-veda, x. 81,4.
† Rig-veda, i. 185,1.
‡ Compare Genesis, i. 1. Here the meaning of the verb *bard* is rendered by "created." It simply conveys the con-

to them by the changes occuring constantly before their eyes in all the departments of nature. And this doctrine is found to be propounded in one of the later hymns of the Rig-veda.* In different other hymns, however, we meet with various speculations about the origin of heaven and earth. The creation of them is sometimes ascribed to Indra, and at other times to other deities, as to Soma, Pûshan, Dhâtri, and Hiranyagarbha. And it is also said that they have received their shape from Tvashtri, and have sprung from the head and the feet of Purusha; and are supported by Mitra, Varuna, Indra, Agni, Savitri, and Soma. Elaborate theories of creation are not to be found in the earlier portions of the hymns;† and the Rishis confess their ignorance of the beginning of all things.‡

ception of mere fashioning or arranging; and does not signify a nihilo creation. There is, however, no trace of the meaning attributed to it by later scholars of a creation out of nothing. According to the Jewish commentators it does not represent so. This idea is altogether a modern idea; and to transfer a modern idea to the mind of Moses is simply absurd.

* Rig-veda, x. 129.
† Rig-veda, i. 67,3; vii. 86,1.
‡ Rig-veda, i. 164,4; x. 81,4.

There is a hymn in the tenth book of the Rigveda of a long antecedent period, of philosophical thought in which we find the conception of a beginning of all things, and of a state, before all things were created. In the beginning there was nothing, no sky, no firmament. No space there was, no life, no time, no difference between day and night. "Darkness there was, and all at first was veiled in gloom profound, as ocean without light." There was only the deep abyss, a chaotic mass, which swallowed every thing. "That one," the poet says, "breathed, and lived; it enjoyed more than mere existence; yet its life was not dependent on any thing else, as our life depends on the air which we breathe. It breathed breathless." Max Müller says "language blushes at such expressions, but her blush is a blush of triumph." The creation is sometimes said to be the manifestation of His will; and a mere evolution of one substance. The idea of the spontaneous evolution of all things out of undeveloped matter, became the foundation of the Sānkhya philosophy. In that remote period we find that the difference between mind and matter was but imperfectly conceived.

The history of mankind clearly shows that man is essentially religious; and the belief in the unseen spiritual world has the foundation in our nature. The high water marks of radical elements of real religion, such as an intuition of God, a sense of human weakness and a feeling of dependence on God, a belief in a divine government of the world, a distinction between good and evil, and a hope of a better life, break forth in the Rig-veda. The earlier portions of the Rik allude very little to a future state; and references to a future state of punishment in the whole body of the Vedas are few and far between; and even these references are obscure. Our ancestors had not contempt for all things beneath the sun, nor had they any dislike for this existence with all its vicissitudes and miseries. They longed for continuation of life, and death by no other cause than by old age; and thought of this life simply as a preparation for a new existence in the world of the departed where to enjoy eternal bliss. They however had no idea of retribution after death; and it was their simple faith that the new existence is merely a continuation of the old age under changed condition. There yet appears a simple faith that the life in this world is not the last of man, but after death he is to go to an abode of happiness above.*

* Prof. Roth, after extracting several passages from the Rik in which a belief in immortality is clearly conveyed, says with

In the ninth and tenth *mandalas* of the Rig-veda, there are some distinct references made to a future life. Besides these there are other texts which intimate the same belief. The consciousness of sin is the prominent characteristic of the religion of the Veda. It is said that the gods take away from man the burden of his sins.* The idea of faith is also found in the Rig-veda,† and that faith is again associated sometimes with true scepticism.‡ In the Veda there are numerous passages in which occurs not only the idea of immortality of the soul, personal immortality, but also personal responsibility after death. That great force,—"We here find, not without astonishment, beautiful conceptions on immortality, expressed in unadorned language with childlike conviction. If it were necessary, we might here find the most powerful weapons against the view which has lately been revived, and proclaimed as new, that Persia was the only birthplace of the idea of immortality, and that even the nations of Europe had derived it from that quarter; as if the religious spirit of every gifted race was not able to arrive at it by its own strength." See Muir's Article on Yama, in the Journal of the Royal Asiatic Society, p. 10.

* Rig-veda, i. 162,22 ; ii. 27,14 ; iv. 12,4 ; v. 82,5 ; vii. 87,7 ; vi. 84,7 ; viii. 48,9 ; x. 25,3.

† Rig-veda, i. 102,2 ; i. 104,6 ; i. 55,5.

‡ Rig-veda, viii. 100,3.

immortality is gained by a son is mentioned in one passage of the Veda;* and one poet prays that he may again see his father and mother after death.† The gods are said to have established the eternal laws of right and wrong; and they punish sin and reward virtue. Morality and religion were already closely connected. But the enjoyments of a future life are most probably to be understood as of a sensual kind.‡ In the Vaidik age even the gods themselves were regarded as subject to the influence of carnal appetites. Some of the hymns attribute to the gods sentiments and passions, such as anger, revenge, and delight in sacrifices; and represent man with all the desires and weaknesses of human nature. Immunity from taxation is held out as the greatest boon to be received in the next world.§ A funeral hymn offered to Agni‖ contains some verses which fully give the views of the writer on the future life. The *pitris*, or ancestral fathers of families, who have departed this life and passed into the heavenly state, are represented as objects of adoration to their

---

* Rig-veda, vii. 56,24.
† Rig-veda, i. 24, 1; compare Atharva-veda, xii. 3,17.
‡ Rig-veda, ix. 113,7 ff.
§ Atharva-veda, iii. 29,3.
‖ Rig-veda, x. 16.

descendants. The fathers are supplicated almost like gods; oblations are offered to them; and they are said to enjoy in company of the gods, a life of eternal felicity.* It is said, that there exist three heavens† of which the *pitris* occupy the highest. In certain passages of the Rig-veda the word *manas* is found to be used for the soul or the animating principle which is never annihilated after the termination of earthly existence.‡ A'*tman* is also employed in several portions of the Rig-veda for the living principle; and in these, the sun is also addressed as the soul of all things changeable or unchangeable.§ Some texts refer indistinctly to the punishment of the wicked.‖ In the Atharva-veda the adjective form of the usual word for hell (*narakn loka*) occurs: and that region is described as the future abode of the illiberal.¶

* Rig-veda, x. 15,16.
† Rig-veda, xviii. 2,48.
‡ Compare Atharva-veda, xviii. 2,23. "Let thy soul (manas) go to its own and hasten to the fathers." The mind (manas) is regarded by the Hindu philosophers as distinct from the soul.
§ Rig-veda, I. 115,1.
‖ Rig-veda, iv. 5,5 ; vii. 104,3 ; ix. 73,8.
¶ xii. 4,36.

From the Rig-veda we learn that the Rishis had conceived the idea of the soul being immortal.[*] There is a prayer of Vasishtha addressed to Varuna (vii. 86) which clearly shows the indestructibility of the spirit. It is scarcely to be expected that in such primitive times they would have very clear ideas on this subject; but it is after all worthy to be noticed that long before Greece and Rome became cultivated communities, and when Europe was the home of uncivilised barbarians, the Rishis had some conception of this doctrine. Modern psychologists cannot teach us more than what was taught by our ancestors some thousand years ago. In the Brāhmaṇas immortality is promised to those who rightly understand and practise the rites of sacrifice without a miss.

There are very few passages in the Brāhmaṇas which proclaim the idea of absorption in the deity such as we find in the Upanishads. But from a passage in the Satapatha-Brāhmaṇa we learn how in the next world the animals and plants would devour them who had made a repast of them in this state of existence unless they were resuscitated to life by the performance of usual ceremonies and

[*] Rig-veda, i. 22.

sacrifices.* The word *prâyaschitta* by which expiation or atonement is implied, does not occur in the songs of the Rig-veda. But it occurs often in the Brâhmanas and Sûtras in the sense of a remedy for repairing a grievance, or averting an evil; and not in the sense of an atonement for a sin committed.

In the Rig-veda Yama is no where described in the same sense as in the later mythology.† He is not represented as a terrible being, but as the ruler of the dead, and of a beneficent character. He grants to the departed souls a resting place where they enjoy eternal happiness. Still Yama is to a certain extent an object of terror and horror. And in a verse of the Atharvan death is said to be the messenger of Yama who conveys the spirits of men to the abode of their forefathers.‡ He is also represented as having two insatiable dogs with four eyes and wide nostrils, which guard the road to his abode.§ The body which the deceased is to assume again in his other existence, cannot be the same which is consumed by the flames, or covered up by the earth; it may not even be similar to it, because he

* xi. 6,1,1 ff.
† Wilson's Vishnu-purâna, p. 207, note 3.
‡ xviii. 2, 27.
§ Rig-veda, x. 14, 10-12.

is to live henceforth in the company of divine spirits, and must be so clothed as to have a right of place among them. And the ancient Indian religion, in complete harmony with the conceptions of the highest gods, and the feeling of an affinity between the human and the divine spirits, plainly teaches that the deceased, purged of all imperfections, is invested by the divine hand with a shining and all glorious spiritual body.* Nowhere in the Rig-veda is any trace discoverable of metempsychosis.† But, on the contrary, it is promised, as the highest reward, that the pious shall again be born in the next world with his identical body.‡ In certain passages a hope is also held out that the family relations will be maintained in the next world.§

How the Vaidik religion gradually changed, may be best known from the Vedas themselves. In a history of ancient Sanskrit literature the Chhandas period is the most interesting and most important in a philosophical point of view. In the Chhandas period, the state of human society being simple, reli-

---

* Roth's article on the Morality of the Vedas in the Journal of the American Oriental Society, iii. p. 343.
† Wilson's Rig-veda, iii. p. xiii. Müller's Chips, i. p. 46.
‡ Rig-veda, iv. 6,1,1; xi. 1,8,6; xii. 8,3,31.
§ Atharva-veda, iii. 8,17; vi. 120,3.

gion was necessarily so. Now the Rishis were the priests of different families to which they imparted religious instructions. The manner in which the idea of religion, however childish, entered the human mind in the infancy of society, is a question too complicated to be dealt with by generalisations from local phenomena. But in the process of time the religion of the Rishis underwent a gradual change. And as soon as we enter into the Mantra period, we observe the gross superstitious character of the Vaidik religion. If we compare the Rik with the other two Vedas, the difference between the Chhandas and Mantra periods becomes apparent and quite intelligible. The religious ideas which began to take root in the minds of the Indo-Aryans of the Mantra period, were sufficiently powerful to make them relinquish all regard for the religion of the Rig-veda. A priesthood was now systematically created. In the Chhandas period, the Rishis used to hold divine service in their families, but now nothing could be done without a priest.

Âsvalâyana says that there were four chief priests, each having three subordinate priests under him. And these sixteen priests are commonly called by the general term of *Ritvix*,* and were chosen

* Roth's Sanskrit and German Dictionary - sub voce *ritvis*.

by the Yajamāna. There were other priests, who of course did not rank as *Ritvis*. The Kaushitakins admit the so-called Sadasyas into the *Ritvi*, who were to superintend all the sacrifices. These priests had peculiar duties to perform, which are prescribed in the Brāhmaṇas. The Adhvaryus had to measure the ground, to build the *vedi*, or altar, to make the sacrificial vessels, to fetch wood and water, to light the fire, to bring the animal and immolate it. And certainly they formed the lowest class of priests. The Udgâtris had to act as the chorus. The peculiar duty of the Hotris was to recite certain hymns in praise of the deities in a loud and distinct voice during the time of sacrifices. The Hotris were by far the most highly educated class of priests. The most ancient name of a professional priest was Purohita; and he was more than a chaplain. He was the counsellor of a chief, and the minister of a king, and his companion, too, in peace and war. The original institution of a Purohita must not be accepted as the sign of a far advanced hierarchical system. The office of a Purohita was however regarded as a divine institution. Vasishtha and Viśvâmitra were the Puro-

where the appellations of the sixteen kinds of priests are given. See also the passage in the Satapatha-Brāhmaṇa, xii. 2 et seq., there referred to.

bitas of king Sudâsa.* The chief occupation of the Purohita was simply to perform the ordinary sacrifices, but his office also partook of a political character. The ancient appellations of the theologians of the Rik as Bahvrichas, those of the Saman as Chhandogas, and of the Yajus as Adhvaryus are to be found in the Samhitâ of the Black Yajus. The Yajus applies the term Adhvaryus to its own adherents, whilst their opponents are designated Charakâdhvaryus. This natural hostility is also clearly shown in a passage of the Samhitâ of the White Yajus.† But this spirit of hostility was not exclusively confined to the different schools of the Yajur-veda; the followers of the Atharva-veda seem to have

---

* Visvâmitra, says Signor de Gubernatis, is to be understood as one of the appellations of the sun, and as both the person who holds the name, and Indra are the sons of Kusika, and they must be brothers. Vasishtha is the greatest of the Vasus, and means Agni, the solar fire, and points out, like Visvâmitra, to the sun. Sudâsa signifies the horse of the sun, or the sun himself. Ancient Indian tradition speaks of both Visvâmitra and Vasishtha as real historical personages. His theory therefore is quite untenable. See the Rivista Orientale, i. pp. 609ff., 678ff.

† Weber's History of Indian Literature, p. 84; Müller's History of Ancient Sanskrit Literature, p. 350.

evinced similar sectarian jealousies towards the adherents of the other Vedas.*

The Brahma had to watch over the three classes of the priests, and to remedy any defect which might vitiate the efficiency of the sacrifice. And the Rig-veda itself, though perhaps in one of its latest portions, recognises the superiority of the Brahma priest. He was, therefore, supposed to know the whole ceremonial, and all the hymns used by the Hotris, Adhvaryus, and Udgâtris. The office of a Brahma priest was not a birth right; but every priest could obtain it by assiduous and unremitting study, great ability, and superior ingenuity. The descendants of such Brahma priests are the Brahmans. The Brahman is regarded with respect and reverence. Great benefits are said to result from the employment of a priest,† and liberality to them is mentioned with approbation;‡ and the highest efficacy is said to result from their intercession.—The term Brahman originally denoted devout worshippers and contemplative sages or poets, who composed hymns in praise of the gods. But after the ceremonial of worship became highly developed

* Weber's Indische Studien, i. p. 236.
† Atharva-veda, iii. 19.
‡ Atharva-veda, i. 125; i. 126; v. 27; v. 30, 12ff; v. 61, 10; i. 27,8; vi. 47, 23ff.

and complicated, and the sacred functions became quite distinct from other occupations, the epithet gradually came to be employed for a minister of religion, and at last it came to signify one particular class of priest with special duties. Then the hierarchy of the Brahmans were completely organised; and that possibly took place towards the close of the Vaidik period. Though now priesthood formed an exclusive caste, which for the most part became hereditary order, yet those among other classes that aspired for sacerdotal functions and privileges, were also admitted to the same order. As a class some of them were intelligent, some unintelligent, some thoughtful, and some as more mechanical instruments at the celebration of ceremonial of worship. A superhuman power appears to be ascribed to the priests;[*] and curses are fulminated against their oppressors.[†] But the comparision of frogs to them imply a total disregard for them and for their functions.[‡] The sacred and divinely consecrated majesty of the priests were not unfrequently attacked by the ungodly; and consequently they had to encounter much difficulty to enforce a due regard which they

[*] Atharva-veda, xix. 9, 12 ; xix. 48,9.
[†] Atharva-veda, v. 17 ; xii. 5.
[‡] Rig-veda, vii. 103.

themselves attached to the performance of religious rites. And we find a long list of condemnatory epithets applied to those persons who were the deniers of the gods, and averse to the rites. The Hotris perform their duties with the Rik, the Udgâtris with the Sâman, the Adhvaryus with the Yajus, and the Brahma with all the first three Vedas.

In the earlier part of the Vaidik times the form of worship was simple and patriarchal; and it was held three times daily simply with hymns and prayers very often accompanied by the fruits of the earth, and the products of the flocks which were offered on the family altars. Then the sacrifices were not left to the charge of the priests; but they were a spontaneous act of devotion, and were neither tedious nor complicated in their minor details. But when in the course of time the priests formed themselves into a privileged class such worships and sacrifices underwent radical changes. All the rites, offerings, oblations and sacrifices were held with the distinct object either to avert an evil or to secure a coveted object by divine intercession, or to propitiate the gods themselves. They were offered either to gain the good will of an offended deity, or through a dread of some. Most of the rites required the sacrifice of a large number of various kind of beasts and birds.

In the Rig-veda the Darsapûrnamâsa and other sacrifices are mentioned; but the modes in which, and the objects for which, they were performed, were all forgotten in the times subsequent to the Vaidik age. They were preserved only as relics of ancient times, and performed in altogether a different manner, and with a different object. At the commencement of the Darsapûrnamâsa sacrifices the Adhvaryus having placed the cows and calves together, have to touch the calves with the branch of a tree. This sacrifice was celebrated at the full and change of the moon. Besides this, we have innumerable names of sacrifices; of which the Râjsuya, Agnihotra, Asvamedha, Somayâga and Purushamedha are by far the most remarkable. The Asvamedha sacrifice was possibly adopted by the Indians from the Scythians, before they crossed the Indus. For the festival, a certain number of animals were tied to posts, but after the customary prayers had been offered up, they were three times led round the sacrificial fire; they were immolated by an axe, and the flesh cut up into fragments, dressed, partly roasted, and partly boiled, and made into balls and eaten. This ceremony was afterwards performed symbolically.* At the performance of the sacrifice, six hundred and nine

* Wilson's Introduction to the Rig-veda.

animals of various descriptions, domestic and wild, according to the deity to whom they were offered, were tied to twenty-one *Yúpas*, or sacrificial posts. Elephants, camels,* buffaloes, birds, porpoises, crocodiles, snakes, and even mosquitoes and worms are named among the animals. The sacrifice of the horse, and that of the cow was common in the earliest periods of the Vaidik ritual. The Bráhmana of the Black Yajus and both the Kalpa and Grihya Sútras distinctly mention the different occasions when cattle should be slaughtered and eaten. It is no less a fact that the meat of cattle was required for the due celebration of scores of other ceremonies; and more particularly for the celebration of the Rájasúya, the Vájapeya, the Asvamedha, the Panchasáradíya sava, and the Súla gava. The proper place for the performance of the latter rite was outside a village or a town, unfrequented by men, and the time was after midnight. The Gomedha was not typical as many would imagine. The Sautrámani ceremony has been incorporated in the Taittirīya-Bráhmana; and there is a wide difference in the treatment which this sacrifice receives in the Satapatha-Bráhmana. In the Sautrámani and Vájapeya rites the offerings of strong spirit formed a promi-

* Compare Sanskrit *krumela*, and Greek καμηλος.

ment part. In the former three animals, a bull being one of them, had to be immolated. And the worshippers were required to partake of the remnant of the oblations. The Gavâmanayana was performed for four days. It formed a part of the Mahâplava, Dvâdaraba, and several other ceremonies; but it did not constitute a distinct rite by itself. The Sarvamedha and Brahmayajna are passed over by the Satapatha-Brâhmaṇa. They find place in the A'ranyaka of the Taittirîyas, but not in their Brâhmaṇas. The Pitrimedha has place in the Brâhmaṇas of the Taittirîyas. The Puruṣamedha required the actual sacrifice of man; and it had for its distinct object the acquirement of independent sovereignty over all created beings. It required forty days for its completion, and more than hundred victims. The sacrifice of human beings formed part of the ancient cultus of India; and there is a strong presumptive evidence that Sunaḥsepha was intended for an actual sacrifice. It is beyond doubt that the Indo-Aryans were familiar with the idea of human sacrifice.[*] And the earliest indication of the rite occurs in the Rig-veda, in the Vâjasaneyî Samhitâ

---

[*] Wilson's Essay on Human Sacrifice in the Veda; Roth, in Weber's Indische Studien, I. pp. 457-464; and ii. pp. 111-123; Weber's History of Indian Literature, p. 84.

of the White Yajur-veda and the Satapatha-Brâhmaṇa. The Aitareya and Taittirîya Brâhmaṇas also refer to it.

The principal object for which the Sâma-veda was composed, is the performance of those sacrifices of which the juice of the Soma plant forms the chief ingredient; and of such sacrifices the most remarkable is the Jyotishtoma, which consists of seven stages; but the celebration of the Agnishtoma alone was deemed obligatory, while other six stages, though adding to the virtue of the sacrificer, were understood as voluntary. The Soma was from the earliest times connected with the religious history of the Indo-Aryans;* and was elevated to the proud position of a god. The Rig-veda is quite replete with its praises; and all the four Vedas contain *mantras* to be recited at all the stages of its manufacture. The high antiquity of this cultus is attested by the references to it to be found in the Persian Avesta.† The plants were gathered by the roots on the hills by moonlight, and brought

* Windischmann's Dissertation on the Soma worship of the Aryans; Whitney's Main Results of the Later Vaidik Researches in Germany; Lassen's Indian Antiquities, i. p. 515; and Roth's articles in the Journal of the German Oriental Society, for 1848 (pp. 216ff.) and 1850 (pp. 417 ff.)

† Plutarch de Isid. et Osir. 46, in which the Soma, or as it is

home in carts drawn by rams; the stalks were bruised and crushed between stones, and placed with the juice in a sieve of goats' hair, and were further pressed and squeezed by the priests' ten fingers ornamented by rings of flattened gold. Finally, the juice mixed with barley, wheat, and clarified butter, is brought into a state of fermentation; and is then drawn off in a scoop, and offered up thrice a day to the gods, and a laddleful is taken for the priests. From the Vaidik descriptions of the effects of the Soma nectar on the gods, to whom it was the most acceptable and delightful oblation, we are to conclude that it was a fermented intoxicating beverage; and this again we assume only from our knowledge of the effects produced by its use in men. The expressed juice of the Soma creeper itself had not either its narcotic property or its keeping quality; but it being diluted with water and mixed with clarified butter, and meals of barley and *niudra*, and at last it being left to ferment in a jar for some days, that it acquired its exhilarating and inebriating effects;* and while it was invested

in Zand, Acoma, appears to be referred to under the appellation of ὅμωμι.

* Stevenson's Sāma-veda, p. 5; Haug's Aitareya-Brâhmana p. 6.

with a sacramental and religious character, it could not be at all manufactured for sale. However the Soma juice in all cases was preserved in a bag of cowskin,

CHAPTER IV.

The Division of the Vedas into Mantras and Bráhmanas—the proper meaning of Sákhá, Charana, and Parishad—the A'ranyakas—the Upanishads and the Distinction between Sruti and Smriti.

The division of the Vedas is two-fold, Mantras and Bráhmanas.[*] Such a division is in fact an indispensable one, separating two different classes of writings, which are related to one another as canonized text on the one hand, and canonized explanation on the other. That part of each Veda which contains the mantras, is called its Samhitá; and this definition applies equally to all the Samhitás except to that of the Black Yajur Veda, in which both the Mantra and the Bráhmana portions are combined. But yet it is to be believed that this Samhitá had a separate Bráhmana annexed to

---

[*] Sáyana says in his Commentary on the Rig-veda: "The definition (of the Veda) as a book composed of mantra and bráhmana, is unobjectionable. Hence A'pastamba says in the Yajnaparibháshá, Mantra and Bráhmana have the name of Veda."

it.* The Brâhmanas stand to the Mantras in the same relation as the Talmud stands to the Mosaic code. The former presuppose the earlier existence of the latter; and the proof that the Mantras are far older than any other portion of Indian literature, is to be found in the character of their language. Though the Mantras and the Brâhmanas were held at a later period to have existed simultaneously, it admits of no question that the Brâhmana portion of each Veda is posterior to some part at least of its Samhitâ; for the former evidently refers to, and contains extracts from the latter. And it scarcely needs be stated that so large a collection of works as both the portions must have been the gradual product of some centuries. Indeed, they represent various conditions and changes of society, various phases of religious belief, and even different periods of language. The difficulty, however, to distinguish these periods, is greatly enhanced by the losses, which these writings may have sustained before they were collected together and preserved in the shape in which we now possess them. The Mantras and the Brâhmanas had to pass through a large

* Müller's History of Ancient Sanskrit Literature, p. 359; and Weber's History of Indian Literature, p. 83.

number of Sâkhâs; and the dimensions which consequently sprung up between these schools, both with respect to the Vaidik texts and their interpretation, was very severe. The Mantras are replete with the thanksgivings of the Rishis composed entirely in verse, whilst the Brâhmanas are in prose. The Mantras were for ages unwritten, and the elliptical style of their composition is the only evidence of their oral transmission.

Most of the Brâhmanas are collective works; and there are old and new Brâhmanas. They were the productions of the schools of the Brahmanic priesthood. Though they are puerile, and in the main tediously prolix, verbose and artificial, yet they are found to contain many important matters both theological and ceremonial. We find in them the oldest rituals, the oldest linguistic expositions, the oldest traditional narratives, and the oldest philosophical speculations all of which are closely interwoven with each other. But they differ widely from one another in point of details; and this is simply owing to the fact that they belong to one or the other of the Vedas. With respect to their origin they occupy a kind of intermediate position between the transition from a simple Vaidik mode of thought to the Brahmanical vagaries. And this transition was brought about solely by the Bráhmaṇas themselves. They were drawn up with a view to enforce various ceremonies and sacrifices, and to illustrate the use of the hymns at them, and the duties of the different classes of priests. The authors, however, completely misunderstood the meaning of the text of the ancient hymns, and suggested the most absurd explanations of the various formulas for the entire sacrificial ceremonials which had of course originally some rational meaning. The number of the old Bráhmaṇas must have been very considerable as every Śákhá consisted of a Samhitá and a Bráhmaṇa. It must not, therefore, be supposed that they were not all composed independently by different authors. Each Bráhmaṇa was included in its own Veda, and was used by its own class of Brahmans. Hence different Bráhmaṇas obtained their names from the different classes of Brahmans. For the Ṛig-veda, the Bráhmaṇas of the Bahvrichas, or the Aitareya, and the Śánkháyana or Kaushítaki; for the Sáma-veda, the Bráhmaṇas of the Chhandogas, or the Tándya, or the Panchavinsa and the Chhándogya; for the White Yajur-veda the Śatapatha-Bráhmaṇa; and for the Atharva-veda the Gopatha-Bráhmaṇa. The Bráhmaṇas of the Ṛik generally enumerate the duties of the Hotris. The Bráhmaṇas of the Sāman specify the duties of the Udgātris; and the Brāhmaṇas of the Yajus confine themselves to the duties of the Adhvaryus.

A Brāhmaṇa was originally a theological tract, and it was so designated, not that it treats of Brahma,* but only because it was composed by the

* Haug's Dissertation on the Original Signification of the word *brahma*:—The word brahma or brahman is the most important word of Hindu theology and philosophy. Brahma occurs twice in the Nighaṇṭavas, as a name for "*food*" (Annachma 2, 7.), and for "*riches*" (dhanaṇāma 2, 10). In Sāyaṇa's commentary on the hymns of the Ṛig-veda it is sometimes explained with reference to this signification, and sometimes in other ways, *e. g.* (1) food, in general; 1, 10, 4: more frequently, sacrificial food as in 4, 22, 1. (2) Performance of the song of the Soma singers, 7, 36, 7, (3) magic, charm, spell, 2,23, 1. (4) ceremonies, having a song of praise as their characteristic. (5) Performance of song and sacrifice 7, 28, 1. (6) The recitation of the Hotri priests. (7) Great, 6, 29, 1. These all seem to point to principal meanings, namely, "food," in particular "*sacrificial food*," and the performance of the song at the sacrifice. The meaning "*devotion*" given to the word "brahma" is quite inapplicable. In the language of the Avesta we find, as far as sound is concerned, an absolutely identical word, namely *baresma*. By it the Parsis understand a regularly cut bundle of twigs tied together with grass, and used at their Fire-ceremonies exactly as the little clipped bundle of kuśa grass is used by Brahmans, at the Soma sacrifices. This latter is called Veda (Aśvalāyana, Srauta-Sūtra 1, 11)

Brahmans. The complete body of the Brāhmaṇas generally gives the impression of having undergone a secondary alteration; and their prevalence constitutes a distinct stage in the progress of the religious history of the Indo-Aryans. As the dogmatical books of the Brahmans they contain a system of tenets, which were of necessity the product of religious practice. If they do not afford an accurate explanation of the principles of belief; they are in other respects very useful for such an exposition, as because they were written with the distinct object of explaining and establishing the whole customary ceremonial of worship. They exhibit, on the whole, a phase in the intellectual history of the Indo- which passes later as a synonym of brahma. This bunch of grass as well as the barsoman has a symbolical meaning. They both represent growing, increase, prosperity. The original meaning of the word was growth. Hence came the meaning "prosperity," "success." As the success of the sacrifice entirely depended upon the holy texts, the chanting, the sacrificial forms and offerings, the word could be used for any one of these essentials. As the chanting of the hymns of praise was the most important of these the word was most frequently employed in this sense. As sacrifice with the Vaidik Indians was the chief means to obtain all earthly and spiritual blessings, but was itself useless without the brahma i. e. success, the latter was at last regarded as the original cause of all beings.

Aryans; but in a literary point of view, they are altogether without any interest. They are in some respects marked by sober reasoning, bold thoughts, lofty expressions, and valuable traditions; but their general characteristics mainly consist in their archaisms, grammatical irregularities, antiquated and tautological style and antiquarian pedantry. In them we find a pantheistic system; and this system was adopted merely for the explanation of the Vaidik deities. There also occur numerous mythical tales of the battles between the Devas and the Asuras, which are to be understood as contests between the Indo-Aryans and the aborigines.* Even there the Brahman, the Kshatriya, the Vaisya and the Súdra are repeatedly named by their proper appellations; and their peculiar offices and relative stations are also clearly discriminated.

The Gopatha-Bráhmana of the Atharva-veda is the Veda of the Bhrigu-angiras; which does not properly belong to the sacred literature of the Indo-Aryans. The primary object of this Bráhmana is to show and establish the importance and also the efficacy of the four Vedas. The first part of it comprises five Prapáthakas; and the other part, called the Uttarabráhmana, consists of more than

* Weber's Indische Studien, i. 166; and ii. 243.

five Prapâṭhakas. The ceremonial is discussed in this book in the same manner as in the other Brâhmaṇas; and there is, indeed, very little difference to be seen between the Gopatha and those Brâhmaṇas. It begins with a theory of the creation of the universe as do the other Brâhmaṇas. It was composed after the schism of the Charakas and the Vâjasaneyins; and we must at any rate assign to it a later date than to the Brâhmaṇas of the other Vedas. The number of the Brâhmaṇas belonging to the Sâma-veda, is eight; and their names are: the Praudha or Mahâ-Brâhmaṇa (i.e., the Panchavinsa) the Shadvinsa, the Sâmavidhi, the A'rsheya, the Devatâdhyâya, the Vansa, the Samhitopanishad, and the Upanishad, which is probably the Chhândogya-Upanishad, and is thus ranked among the Brâhmaṇas. Four of these works have no strong claims to be ranked among the Brâhmaṇas. The A'rsheya is an Anukramaṇî; and the Devatâdhyâya is nothing else. The Vansa forms a part of the Brâhmaṇas themselves. The myths and legends contained in them possess great value. The Tândya Brâhmaṇa, also called the Panchavinsa, contains twenty-five books; and treats exclusively of the Soma sacrifice. This Brâhmaṇa is rich in legends of a mythological character as well as in information generally; but its contents are, upon the whole, of a very dry character. And this work was contemporary with, or even anterior to the flourishing epoch of the Kurupanchālas. The Shadvinsa-Brāhmana is a supplement to the Panchavinsa; and solely treats of expiatory sacrifices and ceremonies of imprecation. The Sāma-vidhān is of a highly artificial character, and presents no feature of interest. It appears that the work, such as it is now extant, has undergone some rearrangement, and belongs to a movement which resulted in the philosophies of Kumārila and Sankara. The subject-matter is nothing else than the descriptions of certain penances and ceremonies which are again of little value in themselves. There is, however, mention of ceremonies some of which are meant for the expiation of not only sins but also of crimes. We are therefore warranted to conclude that in them there are germs of the criminal law of later times.* Burnell assigns to this Brāhmana not a higher antiquity than the fifth Century B.C.† A later Brāhmana probably of modern date, and which is not mentioned by Sāyana, is the Adbhuta-Brāhmana.

* Burnell's Introduction to the Sāma-vidhāna, p. xvii.
† Ibid, p. vii.

The Chhándogya-Bráhmana of the Sáma-veda, of which the Chhándogya-Upanishad constitutes a part, comprises ten Prapáthakas; of these the first two are called the Chhándogya-mantra-Bráhmana, and the rest forms the Chhándogya Upanishad. The Chhándogya Bráhmana contains a mass of highly interesting legends illustrating the gradual development of Brahmanic theology. The Aitareya-Bráhmana originated in the country of the Kurupanchálas and Vasa-Usinaras. This Bráhmana is one of the collections of the sayings of ancient Brahma priests explanatory of the sacred duties of the so-called Hotri priests. Its style is throughout uniform. The greater part of the work appears to have been written by one and the same author; some additions, however, were made afterwards. This Bráhmana and the Sánkháyana or Kaushítaki Bráhmana are closely connected with each other; but there are points of divergence in the distribution of their matter. Though they treat essentially of the same matter, their views of the same question often appear to be antagonistic. The Aitareya contains forty adhyáyas, divided into eight panchikás, but the last ten adhyáyas are but a later addition to it. This work treats chiefly of the Soma sacrifice. The Sánkháyana is a perfectly arranged work, and embraces in thirty adhyāyas the complete sacrificial procedure; and this Brāhmana is a later production than the Aitareya.

The Satapatha Brāhmana is the Brāhmana of the White Yajus. In the Mādhyamdina school the Satapatha consists of 14 kāndas, which are subdivided into 100 adhyāyas (or 68 prapāthakas), 438 brāhmanas, and 7624 kandikās. In the Kānva recension the work consists of seventeen kāndas. This Brāhmana furnishes us with the dogmatical, exegetical, mystical, and philosophical lucubrations of early Brahman theologians and philosophers. A partial examination of this book shows it to be stamped with a character quite in harmony with that of the Aitareya. And again these two works have claims to be recognized as very ancient records of the religious beliefs and rituals, and of the pristine institutions of Indian society. A story in the Satapatha illustrates the relations between the priestly and royal families in the early history of India; and gives us an insight into the policy which actuated the Brahmans to struggle from time to time for political influence. There is also a legend of a deluge, in which Manu alone was preserved for his sanctity and superior wisdom. According to this interesting legend he was not the creator of

K

man, but a representative of an earlier race of men." This Brāhmana may have been edited by Yājnavalkya, but its principal portions, like those of the other Brāhmanas, must have been accumulating for some period before they were all collected and arranged to form the sacred code of a new Charana. We possess the Brāhmanas of the Bahvrichas in the Sākhās of the Aitareyins and the Kaushitakins. But even the Brāhmana of the Kaushitakins which has been transmitted to us as a distinct work, different from the Brāhmana of the Aitareyins, must be regarded as a part of the original bulk of Brahmanical literature, extant among the Bahvrichas. The Brāhmanas of the Taittiriyakas in the Sākhās both of the A'pastambīyas and the Aitareyins, consist of some portions which bear the name of Kathas, and were originally the property of his followers. In the Brāhmanas of the Chhandogas it is apparent that after the main collection was completed, another Brāhmana was added which is called the Shadvinsa. This Brāhmana is supposed to be of very modern date. It speaks not only of temples but also of images of gods.

---

* i. 8,1,1. See also Müller's Ancient Sanskrit Literature, pp. 435 ff; Professor Williams's Indian Epic Poetry, p. 34; and Weber's Indische Studien, i. 160 f.

The Shadvinsa and the Adbhuta are considered to be the only Brâhmanas of the Chhandogas; and they form the most important portion of that class of literature.

The word Sâkhâ is sometimes applied to each of the three original Samhitâs, the Rik, the Yajus and the Sâman. But a Sâkhâ generally signifies an edition of each of the Vedas. There was another class of Sâkhâs, though of a confessedly later date, founded on Sûtras, which seem to have derived their names from historical personages. However there was originally a difference between a Sâkhâ and a Charana; these two words were frequently used as synonyms. Pâṇini speaks of Charanas as comprising a number of followers.* If Sâkhâ is employed in the sense of Charana, this is to be accounted for only by the fact that in India the Sâkhâs existed not as written books, but really in the tradition of the Charanas; each member of a Charana representing and possessing a copy of a book. A Sâkhâ as always a portion of Sruti, cannot properly include law books. But the adherents of certain Sâkhâs might easily adopt a code of institutions, which would go by the name of their Charanas. In the Charanavyûha, a work by Saunac-

* Pâṇini, 4,2,46.

ka, treating of these various schools, five Sákhás are enumerated of the Rig-veda, viz., those of the Sákalas, Vashkalas, A'svaláyanas, Sáukháyanas and Mándúkáyanas. Of the Yajur-veda forty-two or forty-four out of eighty-six are mentioned; and fifteen of which belong to the Vájasaneyins, including those of the Kánvas and Mádhyamdinas. Twelve out of a thousand are said to have once existed of the Sáman; and of the Atharva-veda only nine.

The Atharvanarahasya, a modern treatise on the Atharva-veda, attributing the same number of Sákhás to the Sáma-veda and Atharva-veda, speaks of twenty-one of the Rig-veda, and a hundred of the Yajur-veda. Of all these Sákhás, however, the Rig-veda is now extant only in one; the Yajus in three, and we may say in four; the Sáman perhaps in two; and the Atharvan in one. The only recension in which the Samhitá of the Rig-veda is to be found, is that of the Sakala school. The text of the Black Yajus is extant in the recensions of two schools, that of A'pastamba, and of the Káthaka which belongs to the Charakas; and the White Yajus exists in the recensions of the Mádhyamdinas and the Kanva schools. The Samhitá of the Sáman is preserved in two recensions: in that of the Ranáyaníyas, and probably also of the Kauthamas. The text of the Atharvan is preserved only in the Saunaka school. Each Sâkhâ claimed the possession of the only true and genuine Veda. The discrepancies between these Sâkhâs, however, consisted chiefly in numerous variations of their arrangement of the sacred scriptures; in their subsequent additions or total omissions of texts.

Although the words Sâkhâ and Charana were sometimes used synonymously, yet Sâkhâ properly applies to the traditional text followed as in the phrase *sâkhâm adhite*; and Charana an ideal succession of teachers and pupils. We should then understand by Sâkhâ a traditional recension of any of the Vedas, handed down by different Charanas, or different schools or sects, each strictly adhering to its own traditional text and interpretation. The Brahmans themselves were fully aware of this difference between Sâkhâ and Charana. It is therefore highly probable about the establishment of new Charanas on sacred texts peculiar to themselves, in the event of gross or slight discrepancies in the text of the hymns, as well as differences in the Brâhmanas, as a Sâkhâ always consisted of a Samhitâ and a Brâhmana.

A Parishad means an assembly or a Brahmanic settlement; and the Pârshada might be the title of any book that belonged to a Parishad. The law books lay down the number, age, and qualifications of the Brahmans who must have any claim to compose such an assembly to give decisive opinions on all subjects they would be referred to. The members of the same Charana might become fellows of different Parishads and vice versâ. The real ancestors of the Brahmans are eight in number; and eight gotras are again divided into forty-nine different gotras, and these constitute a still larger number of families. Gotras were confined to Brahmans as well as to Kshatriyas, and Vaisyas; and they depended on a community of blood corresponding to families. Charanas existed among the priestly caste only; and they depended on the community of the sacred texts, and as such they were merely ideal fellowships. All the Brahman families that keep and preserve sacred or sacrificial fire claim a descent from the seven Rishis.* A Brahman is bound by law to know to which of the forty-nine gotras his own family belongs, and in consecrating his own fire he must invoke the ancestors who founded the gotra to which he belongs. Such names as gotra, varga, paksha, and gana are all applied

* Bhriga, Angiras, Visvamitra, Vasishtha, Kasyapa, Atri and Agnati.

in one and the same sense. And these genealogies represent something real and historical.

Of the Bráhmaṇas we find a part called A'ranyakas. By the word A'ranyaka Pániní understands a forester.* If the A'ranyakas were extant during his time, he would have recognised them as parts of the Vedas. The A'ranyakas are so called, according to Sáyaṇa, because they were read in the forest, as if they were the text books of the anchorites, whose devotions were purely spiritual.† Of the A'ranyakas there are four extant, the Brihad, the Taittirīya, the Aitareya, and the Kaushītakī. These, no doubt, belong to a class of Sanskrit writings, the history of which has not yet been properly investigated. Their style is full of strange solecisms.‡ The A'ranyakas were considered to contain the quintessence of the Vedas; and they only treat of the science of Brahma. The A'ranyakas, as an enlargement upon the Bráhmaṇas, presuppose their existence. They are anterior to the Sútras, and likewise they are posterior to the Bráhmaṇas to which they form a kind of appendix.

* वरणान् भजते । 4,2,129.
† Goldstücker's Pániní, p. 129 ; Weber's Indische Studien, v. p. 149.
‡ Cowell's Introduction to the Kaushītakī-Upanishad, p. viii.

The A'ranyakas elucidate the obscure points of religion and philosophy, the nature of God, the creation of the world, and the relation of man to God and subjects of like nature. The names of the authors are unknown to us, because their authorships were disclaimed on the grounds that otherwise the productions would lose all the authority; and also for other reasons that those productions are merely compilations from other works. Modes of modern thought are not wholly wanting in them; though the problems discussed are not, in themselves modern. In one view the A'ranyakas are old, for they exhibit the very dawn of thought; in another, they are modern, for they reflect that dawn with all the experience of days that are past. They also abound in passages which are unequalled in any language, for grandeur, simplicity and boldness.

The original Upanishads, or the Mysteries of Theosophy, had their place in the A'ranyakas and Brahmanas. The most important of them are full of theosophy and philosophy. Max Müller has surmised that the word Upanishad " meant originally the act of sitting down near a teacher, of submissively listening to him," whence it came to mean " implicit faith, and at last truth or divine revelation." It may be supposed with some reason that these works derived their names from the mysteriousness of the doctrines contained in them; and perhaps also from the mystical and obscure manner in which they propound them. It is very probable that, in the time of Pāṇini, the works bearing the name of Upanishads were not then in existence.* Their number is not very considerable. The Upanishads are for the most part short. The ordinary enumeration of them is fifty-one. And besides these there are some others, but they are all spurious. The whole fifty-one were translated into Latin and published by Anquetil du Perron in 1801, under the title of "Oupnekhat" or "Theosophia Indica." His translations were largely from a Persian version prepared at the order of Dārā Shakoh. The various systems of Hindu philosophy have their basis in the Upanishads, though quite antagonistic in their character. Most of the modern Upanishads are really the works of Gaudapāda, Sankara, and other philosophers. Founders of new sects composed numerous other Upanishads of their own as the ancient ones did not suit their purpose.† The original Upanishads must ever occupy a prominent

* Goldstücker's Pāṇini, p. 141.

† Ward, A View of the History, Literature and Mythology of the Hindoo, ii, p. 51.

place in the sacred literature of the Indo-Aryans. The theological and philosophical speculations they contain are sublime emanations of the human mind. They are the most ancient monuments of philosophical conceptions, and as such they are, far more advanced both in the depth and loftiness of their ideas and opinions than any of the Greek schools prior to Socrates, only except to that of Elea. They, as the case may be, contributed much towards the formation of the civil and domestic polity, and directed the whole tone of moral ordinances. They are considered with some show of reason as the highest authorities on which the various systems of philosophy are said to rest. The Vedânta philosopher seeks some warranty for his faith in the Veda; and the Sankhya, the Vaiseshika, the Nyâya and the Yoga philosophers profess to find in the Upanishads some authority for their opinions though there is no ground of harmony between them; the chief object of the Upanishads being to unfold the darkest points of philosophy and religion, to discuss the creation of the world, to descant on the nature of God, and to elucidate the relation of man to God and the like. There is however not to be found any systematic uniformity in the Upanishads; but as regards the range of ideas and the style the case place in the sacred literature of the Indo-Aryans. The theological and philosophical speculations they contain are sublime emanations of the human mind. They are the most ancient monuments of philosophical conceptions, and as such they are, far more advanced both in the depth and loftiness of their ideas and opinions than any of the Greek schools prior to Socrates, only except to that of Elea. They, as the case may be, contributed much towards the formation of the civil and domestic polity, and directed the whole tone of moral ordinances. They are considered with some show of reason as the highest authorities on which the various systems of philosophy are said to rest. The Vedânta philosopher seeks some warranty for his faith in the Veda; and the Sankhya, the Vaiseshika, the Nyâya and the Yoga philosophers profess to find in the Upanishads some authority for their opinions though there is no ground of harmony between them; the chief object of the Upanishads being to unfold the darkest points of philosophy and religion, to discuss the creation of the world, to descant on the nature of God, and to elucidate the relation of man to God and the like. There is however not to be found any systematic uniformity in the Upanishads; but as regards the range of ideas and the style the case is the substance of the universe; that the creation is nothing else than a multiplication and development of Himself: and the universe is to Him what the butter is to the milk, or as vapour rising from the ocean, condensing and falling back to the source whence it came. The Upanishads are not the works of the same author, or even of the same age. They inculcate pantheism of one kind or another. The theory of no two of them can be regarded precisely the same. Some of them abound in speculations, much after the fashion of development philosophers, on the physical primeval element of the universe, and whatever is, on the impulse of the moment accepted as a first principle, is announced to be Brahma or God. The great teachers of this Parâ, or superior knowledge, were Kshatriyas, and Brahmans are merely represented as becoming pupils of the great Kshatriya kings. The Kshatriya mind first followed out these bold speculations; and we can scarcely escape this conclusion when we add to this the remarkable fact that the Gâyatrî itself, the most sacred symbol in the universe, is a hymn by an author, not a Brahman but a Kshatriya.[*] The Upanishads abound in descriptions not merely of carnal observances; but also of ob-

[*] Viśvâmitra.

scenities still worse and grosser than Jayadeva's battles of love.

Almost all the Upanishads are small books, save the Brihadáranyaka, which constitutes the last five prapáthakas of the fourteenth book of the Satapatha-Bráhmana. This Upanishad is divided into six chapters, and each chapter is again sub-divided into different bráhmanas. The Brihadáranyaka is the conclusion of the Vájasaneyi-Samhitá. It consists of seven chapters, or eight lectures. The Taittiríya-Upanishad is a part of the Taittiríyáranyaka of the Black Yajus. It is divided into two parts as Sikshá-vallí and Brahmánanda-vallí. We trace in it the germ of the Vedánta system. The Taittiríyáranyaka is older than the Brihadáranyaka. It shows a strange medley of post-Vaidik ideas and names. The Aitareyáranyaka forms a work by itself; the second and third parts of which form the Bahvricha-Upanishad. The Aitareya is more speculative and mystical than legendary or practical. There is another A'ranyaka within a Sákhá of the Rig-veda, which is called the Kaushitaká-ranyaka in three adhyáyas of which the third constitutes the Kaushítaki-Upanishad. There are no A'ranyakas for the Sáma-veda, nor for the Atharva-veda. The A'ranyakas derive their authority

1.

from Sruti. Sâyana states that the Taittirîya-Upanishad comprises three parts, and they go by the names of Samhitî, Yâjnikî, and Vârunî; of these the last is the most important, because it teaches the knowledge of the divine self. The Aitareya is included in the second A'ranyaka of the Aitareya-Brâhmana. It contains three chapters. The Taittirîya and Aitareya resemble each other in a great measure. The Svetâsvatara is comparatively modern. In fact it does not belong to the series of the more ancient Upanishads. It was composed after the publication of the Vedânta and Sânkhya; and is a compound of Vedânta pantheism and the Sânkhya duality. The Vâjasaneyi-Upanishad is very short. It is composed only of eighteen *srutis*; and forms an index to the Vâjasaneyi-Samhitâ. The Talavakâra, or Kena,-Upanishad, which is one of the shortest, and one of the most philosophical treatises of this kind, puts in clearer language, perhaps, than any other Upanishad, the doctrine that the true knowledge of the Supreme Spirit consists in the consciousness which man acquires of his complete inability to understand it, since the human mind being capable only of comprehending finite objects, cannot have a knowledge of what is infinite. The Kena is included in both the Atharvas and the Sâman. The Kaṭha has always been considered as one of the best Upanishads; and it must be admitted on the point of its elevation of thought, elegance of expression, beauty of imagery, and ingenuous fervour, few stand parallel to it. It consists of two adhyâyas, each of which contains three vallis. The first part is quite independent. But the second is composed almost entirely of Vaidik quotations, which prove more in detail the doctrine enunciated in the first. It is on this account that both parts are with some reason taken as two distinct Upanishads. There can be no doubt as to the second part being later than the first, and this is clear from several other, particularly linguistic, reasons. But Dr. Weber is of opinion that the Kaṭha originally closed with the third valli.[*] This Upanishad treats; first, of the highest object of man; second, the First Cause of the world and his attributes; third, the connexion of this Cause with the world. These questions are mooted in the different chapters in a manner which is quite peculiar to the Upanishads in general. The standpoint of the Kaṭha is however on the whole that of the scholastic doctrines of the Vedânta philosophy. We cannot give the same credit to the

[*] Weber's Indische Studien, ii. pp. 197-200 ff.

philosophy as to the form of the Katha; there is scarcely any link connecting the thoughts, so that they rather show that it is plainly a compilation than the production of an original and devout thinker. According to the Katha, the knowledge of Brahma hangs upon a process of thinking, i.e. it is derived from philosophy, and not from revelation. The Prasna, one of the Upanishads in the Atharva-veda, is divided into six chapters, each of which attempts to solve a distinct question. From the first question we arrive at the knowledge of the relation that exists between Prajâpati and the creatures, the period of creation, and the manner in which Prajâpati is to be worshipped. The description is altogether mythological and symbolical, and does not show any well defined thought. The second recounts his relation to individual bodies. By the third question we should understand that life, when produced from the soul, is said to be composed of the five vital airs, by whose regular actions the functions of the body are sustained. The remaining part of this question furnishes us with a specimen of the anatomical and physiological knowledge of the author; and a bold attempt to apply the functions observed in the microcosm of the human body to the macrocosm of the world.

The fourth question is free from mythological embellishments, and gives the substance of the doctrines of the entire Upanishad.

The Mundaka-Upanishad contains three mundakas, each of which is sub-divided into two khandas. There are two sciences, according to the first mundako, the aparā and the parā. The former is founded on the four Vedas and the six Vedāngas; the latter refers to Brahma, that Being who is incomprehensible to the organs of action and intellect, and without qualities. We find a mention of the Vedānta and Yoga in this Upanishad. "It would almost be a contradiction in terms, to say that the Mundaka is a section of the Atharva-veda, which it condemns, along with the others, as inferior science. And if it must be referred to a post-Vaidik age, it would be difficult to affirm that it was composed before the age of Buddha."* The identity between the Katha, Prasna, and Mundaka appears not merely in the mode of explanation, but also in the images and in entire passages, and is very remarkable. More particularly is this the case between the Mundaka and Katha than between the Mundaka and Prasna Upanishads. Which of these Upanishads was the original, or what relation they bear to other sources, can hardly be decided,

* Banerjee's Dialogues.

This much, however, may be said, that the Praśna bears every mark of compilation. The Māṇḍūkya has only twelve slokas. In these slokas the meaning of the mystical syllable *Om* is unravelled. This Upanishad is taken from various sources. From it, the contents having been stripped of their abstruse phraseology, we are to understand that Brahma comprehends all things, both objects of perception and those that are beyond the reach of perception. Brahma has four modes of existence, the waking state, the state of dreaming, the state of profound sleep, and a fourth state quite different from any of the former; this state is indescribable, in which all manifestations have ceased, it is blissful and without duality. The Māṇḍūkya is one of the latest among the Upanishads which show the pristine notion of the Infinite Spirit wholly uncontaminated by sectarian views. The order, in which the state of Brahma's existence is described, exhibits, on the whole, a very profound mode of thought. In the Chhāndogyopanishad a number of most curious modes of upāsanās is prescribed. One of these devotions is so grossly obscene and filthy that I must refrain from translating or reproducing it here. The Bahvrichas placed Atman or the Self at the beginning of all things. The Taittirīyakas speak of Brahma as true, omniscient and infinite. Calling Brahma as neuter, they give proofs of their having been impressed with the idea of a Power. It was decidedly an era in the history of the human intellect when the apparent identity of the Self in the masculine, and Brahma in the neuter, was for the first time clearly established. The Chhandogas speak of a *Sat*, or a Being which had the eagerness to be many. The Atharvanikas speak of the Creator as *Akshar*; and it is very doubtful whether they had with this word any idea of Element or of the Indestructible. The term used by the Vajasaneyins is *Avyákrita*, or the Undeveloped. The Upanishads are the principal parts of the Vedas. Of all the Vaidik works, they were the last composed.

The Vaidik Samhitâs, Brâhmanas and Upanishads are known by the name of *Sruti*. Except the Vedas, all the other works of the Vaidik period, are called *Sûtra*. The Sûtra period is very important in the Vaidik age; and forms no doubt the connecting link between the Vaidik and the later Sanskrit. The distinction between *Sruti* and *Smriti*, had been established by the Brahmans prior to the rise of Buddhism, or prior to the time when the style of the Sûtras gained admittance into Indian literature. The name of Smriti occurs for the first time in the Taittiríyáranyaka,* though it is used there in the sense of Sruti. That Smriti has no claim to an independent authority, but derives its sanction from its relation to Sruti, is to be understood by its very name which means *recollection*. In the Sûtras the distinction between Sruti and Smriti is plainly marked out. We find the distinction as shown in the Anupada-Sûtra.† And also in the Nidána-Sûtra ancient tradition is mentioned under the name of Smriti.‡

---

* Taittiríyáranyaka, i. 1,2.
† Anupada-Sûtra, ii. 4.
‡ Nidána-Sûtra, ii. 1.

CHAPTER V.

The Peculiarities of the Sûtras—the Vedângas—the Origin and General Character of the Prâtisâkhyas—the Anukramanis—the Parisishtas—the Origin of Buddhism—the Knowledge of Writing in ancient India.

The Sûtra is the technical name given to aphoristic rules, and also to works consisting of such rules. The importance of the term may be conceived from the fact, that the groundworks of the whole ritual, grammatical, metrical, and philosophical literature of India are indited in the aphoristic style, which exhibits one of the peculiarities of Indian authorship. Though there is no clear evidence as to the cause which gave birth to this peculiarity in Sanskrit composition; the method of instruction followed in ancient India renders it probable that these Sûtras were so composed, and were intended to accelerate the studies of the pupil who had to learn simply by heart. But it is equally probable that this method of schooling itself gained ground because of the scarcity or clumsiness of the materials used for writing purposes, and in consequence of the expediency of economising this material as far as could be possible. The Sûtra works are all brief and systematic, and enigmatical. Conciseness is the principal object which guided the authors of the Sûtra works. Even the bare simplicity of the design vanishes in the perplexity of the structure. To acquire mastery over the Sûtra works is next to impossible, without the help of the key which is found in separate Sûtras called Paribhâshâ. Notwithstanding this key the pupil also must be in possession of the laws of the so-called Anuvritti and Nirvritti. They are certainly one of the most curious sorts of literary composition that the human mind ever produced; and if altogether worthless in an artistic point of view, it is remarkable that the Indo-Aryans should have fabricated this most difficult form, and adopted it as the most convenient vehicle of expression of every branch of learning.

The studied brevity of the Sûtras renders them in a high degree obscure and ambiguous. Notwithstanding the key to their interpretations, there are to be found many seeming contradictions. The Sûtras bewilder even a scholar, and puzzle him at the very threshold in a labyrinth of symbols and abbreviations. The Sûtra works contain the quintessence of all the knowledge which the Brâhmanas themselves had accumulated during many centuries of study and reflection. The cut and dry style of the Sûtra is so peculiar to India that it allows of no comparison with the style of composition of other countries in the early times when they were composed.

We have to search for the Vedânga doctrines in all their originality and authenticity in the Brâhmaṇas and the Sûtras; and not in those barren tracts which are now known by the name of Vedângas. The Vedângas are not parts of the Vedas themselves; but supplementary to them, and, in the form in which we possess them, are not, wholly genuine; and in fact are of little importance. They are, however, auxiliary books for understanding the Vedas. All those works were written with an object of their being practical; and they exhibit quite a novel phase in the literature of the ancient Indians. Their authors were not inspired, and the style which they employed to subserve their purpose, was business-like on the whole. Manu calls them Pravachanas," a title which is usually applied to the Brâhmaṇas. We find the earliest mention of the six Vedângas in one of the Brâhmaṇas of the

---

* Manu, iii. 194.

Sâman, but their names are not given there.[*] Yâska (Nir. i. 20) quotes only the Vedângas generally without particularizing any of the six Vedângas. The number of the six Vedângas occurs in the Charaṇavyûha, and also in Manu (iii. 185) and the Chhândogyopanishad. A very vivid statement as to the rational character of the Vedângas is given in the Brihadâraṇyaka and its commentary. The Muṇḍakopanishad gives us the entire number of the Vedângas.

The first Vedânga is called the Sikshâ which, according to Sâyaṇa, who lived in the 14th century A.D.,[†] comprises rules regarding letters, accents, quantity, organs, enumeration, delivery, and euphonic combinations. We have another tract on Sikshâ, called the Mâṇḍûkî Sikshâ. But this also is probably a later production of the Sûtra period, and it is of much importance as it bears the name of another Charaṇa of the Rig-veda, the Mâṇḍûkâyaṇa. The rules of the Sikshâ had formerly a place in the seventh book of the Taittirîyâraṇyaka. Sâyaṇa is found to take the same view in his commentary on the Samhitâ-Upanishad. It is supposed

---

[*] Shadvinsa-Brâhmaṇa, iv. 7.

[†] Wilson's Rig-veda, i. p. xlviii; Müller's Sanskrit Researches, p. 197.

that they lost this place by the appearance of the Pratisakhyas. But nothing is found in the Pushpa-Sūtra of Gobhila to prove this.

The second is Chhandas which treats of metre. The work of Pingalanāga on Chhandas, which is frequently quoted under the title of Vedānga, is not of great antiquity. Some suppose Pingala was the same as Patanjali, the author of the Mahā-bhāshya.* But the identity of Pingala and Patanjali is far from being probable. It is not surprising that Pingala does not confine himself to the metres of Sanskrit, but gives also rules bearing on the metres of Prākrita; and even Kātyāyana-vararuchi, the author of the Vārttikas on Pāṇini, the great Father of Sanskrit Grammar, is said to have written a Prākrita grammar. It must be admitted that the treatise of Pingala on Chhandas was one of the last books that were included in the Sūtra period. Prof. Wilson supposes it to be scarcely regarded as belonging to this period. But it is no valid objection that those rules which refer to the Chhandas are not observed in the Vedas. On any ground, however we cannot exclude it from this period altogether. Pingala is quoted as an authority on metre in the Parisishtas. We learn from Shadguru-

* Colebrooke's Miscellaneous Essays, II. p. 63.

M

śishya that Pingala was the younger brother, or at least, the descendant of Pâṇini. The first Prâtiśâkhya contains a section on metre which is far more valuable than this utterly unimportant book known by the name of Chhandas.

The third is Vyâkaraṇa. The Hindus paid much attention to the science of Grammar. Pâṇini throws much light on the Vaidik Sanskrit; and his grammar consists of eight adhyâyas, each adhyâya comprising four pâdas, and each pâda a number of sûtras. The latter amount on the whole to 3996 sûtras or aphorisms composed with the symbolic brevity of the most concise memoriæ technica; but three, perhaps four, of them did not originally belong to the work. The arrangement of these rules differs completely from what a European would expect in a grammatical treatise, for it is based on the principle of tracing linguistic phenomena, and not concerned in the taxonomy of the linguistic material, according to the so-called parts of speech. In a general manner, Pâṇini's work may be called a natural history of the Sanskrit language. The sûtras are all made up of the driest technicalities. Pâṇini records such phenomena of the language as are exceedingly interesting and useful from a grammatical point of view. Words which he has treated of are also of historical and antiquarian interest. The perfect phonetic system on which Pāṇini's grammar is built, is without a shadow of doubt, borrowed from the Prātiśākhyas; but the source of Pāṇini's purely grammatical doctrines must be sought for elsewhere. To fix the age in which Pāṇini lived, is a task we are incapable of performing; as many of the Indian authors shine, to use the words of a well-known Sanskrit scholar, like fixed stars in India's literary firmament, but no telescope can discover any appreciable diameter. However it must be of some interest to know whether that Patriarch of Sanskrit Philology is likely to have lived before the death of Buddha, or after this event. According to the views expressed by Prof. Goldstücker, it is probable that Pāṇini lived before Buddha, the founder of the Buddhist religion, whose death took place about 543 B.C.; but that a more definite date of the great Grammarian has but little chance of being obtained in the actual condition of Sanskrit philology. It is a matter of great surprise that Müller holds Pāṇini to be anterior to Yāska. But Yāska is noticed by Pāṇini himself;[*] and therefore we must believe that Pāṇini was posterior to Yāska.

---

[*] Pāṇini, ii. 4.63: यस्कादिभ्यो गोत्रे । See also Lassen's Indian Antiquities, i. pp. 864-865.

The Mahâbhâshya is not a full commentary on Pâṇini, but with a few exceptions, only a commentary on the Vârttikas, or critical remarks of Kâtyâyana on Pâṇini. From circumstantial evidence, Prof. Goldstücker has proved that Patanjali wrote his Mahâbhâshya between 140 and 120 B. C.[*] Kâtyâyna, the critic of the great Grammarian, is most likely the same with the Kâtyâyana who wrote the grammatical treatise called the Prâtiśâkhya of the White Yajus. Goldstücker has shown that he could not have been a contemporary of Pâṇini, as is generally supposed. He has also proved that this Kâtyâyana was a cotemporary of Patanjali; and probably being the teacher of the latter, he must have lived in the beginning of the second century before Christ. Kâtyâyana completed and corrected Pâṇini's Grammar; and his Vârttikas show a more wide and profound knowledge of Sanskrit than the work of Pâṇini himself.

There are two different books on grammatical subjects written in the period anterior to Pâṇini; the Uṇâdi-Sûtras and the Phiṭ-Sûtras of Sântanâchârya. As to when Sântana's Phiṭ-Sûtras were composed, we are perfectly in the dark. Pâṇini does not presuppose a knowledge of them; and the grammatical

[*] Pâṇini: His Place in Sanskrit Literature, p. 235ff.

terms employed by Sântana are quite different from those adopted by Pânini. Although those sûtras treat simply of the accents, and the accents such as used in the Vaidik language; the subject of Sântana's work compels us to suppose that he was anterior to Pânini. "The Unâdi-Sûtras are rules for deriving, from the acknowledged verbal roots of the Sanskrit, a number of appellative nouns, by means of a species of suffixes, which, though nearly allied to the so-called *krits*, are not commonly used for the purposes of derivation." . . . "A peculiarity of all words derived by an unâdi is, that, whether they be substantives or adjectives, they do not express a general or indefinite agent, but receive an individual signification, not necessarily resulting from the combination of the suffix with a verbal root."* The Unâdi-Sûtras we now possess, are not in their original form. It was not the purpose of the author to give a complete list of all the unâdi words, but merely to collect the most important of them. In fact these were originally intended for the Veda only, and subsequently enlarged by adding rules, on the formation of non-Vaidik words. The Unâdi-Sûtras may have been composed by Sâkatâyana, a Sûdra and a follower of Buddha. A very

* Aufrecht's Unâdi-Sûtras, p. v.

interesting passage in Virâla's Rupamâlâ, distinctly ascribes the authorship of the Unâdi-Sûtras to Vararuchi; and who is no other than Kâtyâyana.

The fourth Vedânga is the Nirukta of Yâska, which is a sort of commentary on the Nighantus. The Nirukta frequently refers to the Brâhmanas, and brings forward various legends, such as those about Devâpi (xi. 10) and Visvâmitra (ii. 24). Yâska furnishes us also with the names of no less than seventeen interpreters who had preceded him;[*] and whose explanations of the Veda are generally in conflict. The Nighantus comprise a vocabulary of obsolete terms. The first three sections are made up of lists of synonymous words. The two other sections consist of mere lists of words of different meanings. The Nighantus and Nirukta are closely connected; the former is older than the latter. If the Nirukta belongs to Yâska; the Nighantus also could not have proceeded from his pen. To the Nirukta we are inclined to attribute a very high antiquity; it belongs to the oldest part of Sanskrit literature excepting the Vaidik writings, and to an already far advanced period of grammar and interpretation. The Nirukta consists of three parts. The first comprises five short chapters, the second or

[*] Roth's Illustrations, pp. 221 f.

Naigama consists of six long chapters, and the third or Daivata eight more. In this work we find the first fundamental notions of grammar.

Yáska prefixed the Nighantus to his own work, the Nirukta, in which he throws light on the obscurities of the Vedas. When this work of Yáska was composed, and even at a much earlier period, it is obvious that the sense of most of the Vaidik words had been completely confounded. This clearly appears from the fact of such works as the Nighantus and Nirukta being written at all. The Nirukta together with the Prátisákhyas and the grammar of Pánini supplies the most important information on the growth of grammatical science in India. Yáska is wholly uninformed of algebraical symbols such as are contained in Pánini. The introduction to the Nirukta, which presents a full sketch of a grammatical and exegetical system, brings to our knowledge the views of Yáska and his predecessors; and it is in this manner we are able to establish a complete comparison of these older grammarians with Pánini.

The fifth is the Kalpa, or the Ceremonial. The accounts of the sacrifices are found in the Kalpa works. But they are merely extracted from the Bráhmanas. The composition of the Kalpa-Sútras is in some respects an important event in the Vaidik history. Though they do not claim to be Smritis, still they are enumerated amongst the Svádhyáyas. The Kalpa-Sútras must have been drawn up for the easy reference of the priests, who would otherwise have to grope in the dark through the liturgical Samhitas and Bráhmanas for the disjecta membra of the sacrificial and other rites. Thus there are the Kalpa-Sútras for the Hotri priests by Áśvaláyana and Sankháyana; for the Adhvaryus by Ápastamba, Baudháyana and Kátyáyana; and for the Udgátris by Látyáyana and Dráhyáyana. The Kalpa-Sútras are divided into three classes, as Srauta, Grihya, and Sámayáchárika; the first prescribes the especial Vaidik ceremonials, such as those are to be celebrated on the days of new and full moon. The rites according to the Srauta-Sútras can be performed by rich people and no other; and have therefore been made obligatory only under certain restrictions. The second enjoins the domestic rites performed at various stages of the life of the Indians from birth to death. The Grihya-Sútras give general rules which are to be observed at marriages, at the birth of a child, on the day of naming the child, at the tonsure and investiture of a boy, and at the time of and after a death. Indeed, the Grihya-Sútras contain all the rules bearing on those principal and purificatory ceremonies which are included under the general name of *samskára*.* The rites and ceremonies according to the Grihya are called Pákayajna. By a Pákayajna we are to understand a piece of wood placed on the fire in the hearth, an oblation made to the gods, and gifts bestowed on the Brahmans. The third regulates the daily observances of the twice born. The rules of the Sámayáchárika-Sútras are rather based on secular authority than sacred. They describe the duties of a boy as a Brahmachária or catechumen, in the house of his preceptor. They regulate the proper diet of a Brahman; what food is allowable and what not; what days should be allotted for fasting; and what penance ought to be performed for not observing duty. They decide, in a great measure, the duties and rights of kings and magistrates, civil rights, and even rules of social politeness. The Drahyáyana belongs to the school of the Ránáyaníyas. It differs but slightly from the Látyáyana, and treats, on the whole, of the same identical matter. The Látyáyana belongs to the school of the Kauthumas. Its first seven prapáthakas contain the injunctions applicable to all the Soma sacrifices; the 8th and part of the 9th prapáthaka

---

* Cf. Wilson's Dictionary, s.v.

treat of the *sûktas*; the remainder of the 9th of the *aktâas*; and the 10th of the *sattra*, or sessions.

The Kalpa-Sûtras mark a new period of literature; and contributed also to the extinction of the numerous Brâhmanas. At any rate, the introduction of a Kalpa-Sûtra was the introduction of a new book of liturgy. The Srauta and Grihya-Sûtras are of much greater moment than the Sâmayâchârika. The Grihya and Sâmayâchârika-Sûtras have generally been confounded; but the Brahmans draw a line of demarcation between the two, the Grihya-ceremonies, being performed by the married house-holder with no other purpose but for the benefit of his family. The Srauta-Sûtras mean the whole body of the Sûtras, the source of which can be traced to the Smriti; while those of the Smârta-Sûtras have no such source. The main difference between the two lies not in their matter; but in the age and the style of composition. The Srauta-Sûtras deal with the grand and public religious ceremonies, rites and sacrifices. The Kalpa-Sûtras, composed by A'svalâyana for the Hotri priests, were intended both for the Sâkala-sâkhâ and Vâshkala-sâkhâ, and again they occasionally refer to the other Charanas. Both the Grihya and Sâmayâchârika-Sûtras are included under the common title of Smârta-Sûtras, in opposition to the Srauta-Sûtras. The former derived their authority from Smriti, and the latter from Sruti. The Sâmayâchârika-Sûtras are sometimes called Dharma-Sûtras, and seem to have been the source of the Dharma-sâstra. The Kalpa-Sûtras are a complete system of ritualism, which have no other object in view than to arrange the whole method of the sacred ceremonial with all the precisions demanded for acts done in the presence of the deities and to their honor. It is not yet proved that the Kalpa-Sûtras are part of the Vedas; and in fact, it is impossible to prove it. They were composed contemporaneously with Pâṇini. We are here to observe once for all that there are ten sûtras of the Sâma-veda; and these Sâma-Sûtras do not all treat of the Kalpa or the Ceremonial. The Kalpa-Sûtras of the Taittirîya-Samhitâ represented or countenanced, more than other Kalpa-Sûtras, the tenets and decisions of the Mîmânsa philosophers. During the time of the composition of these Sûtra works, the whole system of social organisation was developed, and the distinction of caste was fully established. On examining the Sûtra works, and especially the Grihya-Sûtras we find that women have no right to the use of the Vedas. Although women are debarred from reading the Vedas; yet from the same source we obtain the information that a husband in conjunction with his wife may perform sacrifices and other rites. During the time of sacrifices women are allowed to recite mantras as told by their husbands; but they are scrupulously and entirely denied the knowledge of God.

The sixth and last of the Vedāngas is Jyotisha. Works of astronomy were very scanty. The only copy we possess, is comparatively modern, and its literature is very meagre. Its main object is to offer such information about the heavenly bodies as are useful in fixing the days and hours of the Vaidik sacrifices, and not to teach astronomy.

Most of the Vedāngas were composed by Saunaka and his pupils, Kātyāyana and Āśvalāyana. We obtain some information about Kātyāyana from the Kathāsaritsāgara, the encyclopædia of legends by Somadeva Bhatta of Kashmir. But after all we are to reject it as an episode in the story of a ghost. Somadeva composed it for the entertainment of the grand-mother of Sri Harshadeva, king of Kashmir, who ascended the throne of that country in 1059, and reigned, according to Abu'l-fazel, only 12 years; and consequently it must have been written between 1059 and 1071, or a few years earlier. The Kathásaritságara is supposed by many to be the sheet-anchor of Indian chronology.

The Prátisákhyas were designated under the title of the Charanas; because they were the property of the readers of certain Sákhás. They are really a subdivision of the Párshada books. The Párshada is another title often applied to the Prátisákhyas. The existing representatives of the Prátisákhyas, in all probability, are posterior to Pánini;[*] and most of their rules are intended to supply the deficiencies in the Sútras of that Grammarian. The Prátisákhyas are nothing else than "theological and mystical dreams;" but they are not altogether destitute of exegetical as well as critical value. There is no doubt that they were written for practical purposes; and their style is free from cumbrous ornaments and unnecessary subtleties. Their object is to teach rather than to entertain. A great number of authors are referred to in the Prátisákhyas; whose opinions, with general precepts, are found in them. Though we do not possess the works of these earlier authors, yet we may fairly assume that their favourite doctrines were treasured up originally in the shape of Prátisákhyas. These writings contain rules on ac-

[*] Goldstücker's Pánini, p. 185ff.

cent, Sandhi, on the permutation of sounds, the lengthening of the vowels in the Vedas, pronunciation, the various pâthas of the Vedas, &c. The Kuladharmas could not be called Prâtiśâkhyas; but they might claim the title of Charana or Pârshada.

The rules of the Prâtiśâkhyas were by no means intended for written literature; they were merely a guide in the instructions of pupils who had to learn the text of the Vedas by heart. According to the representation of the Prâtiśâkhyas there are three modes of writing the Vedas, viz., the Samhitâ-pâtha, the Pada-pâtha, and the Krama-pâtha. The Samhitâ-pâtha means the mode of writing with observance of the rules of permutation; the Pada-pâtha separates single words. And the Krama-pâtha is two-fold, viz., the Varna-krama and Pada-krama. The Varna-krama always doubles the first consonant of a group of consonants; and the Pada-krama takes two words of the sentence together, and always reiterates the second of them with a following one. Of all the Prâtiśâkhyas of the numerous Vaidik Samhitâs, the Prâtiśâkhyas belonging to the Śâkala-śâkhâ is by far the most complete.

There is another class of Sûtra works called the Anukramaṇîs. The Anukramaṇî to the Rig-veda is by far the most perfect. It is called the Sarvânukramaṇî; it specifies the first words of each hymn, the number of verses, the name and family of the author, the name of the deity to whom hymns are addressed, and the metre of every verse. Before this was completed there were separate indices for each of the subjects. It is said to have been composed by Kâtyâyana. Shaḍguruśishya, in his Vedârthadîpikâ, states that there were five other Anukramaṇîs of Saunaka long before the Sarvânukramaṇî was composed. We have then, on the whole, seven Anukramaṇîs to the Rig-veda. The Brihaddevatâ being very voluminous, is not reckoned at all among the body of the Anukramaṇîs. The Brihaddevatâ of Saunaka, composed in epic metre, contains an enumeration of the gods invoked in the hymns of the Rig-veda; and it further supplies much valuable mythological information about the character of the deities of the Vedas. It is not unreasonable to suppose, judging from the style of composition of the Brihaddevatâ, that it was recast by a later writer. Dr. Kuhn infers from a passage in Shaḍguruśishya's commentary, that not Saunaka, but Âsvalâyana was the author of the Brihaddevatâ. This inference, however, is not supported by sufficient evidence. Saunaka writes, in mixed slokas, and breaks in many cases the laws of metre. Kâtyâyana writes in prose much after the fashion of the later Sûtras. The relation between Saunaka and Kâtyâyana was very intimate; and both of them belonged to the same Sâkhâ. But it is probable that Saunaka was anterior to Kâtyâyana.

The Rig-veda hymns are arranged according to two methods; the one having regard to the material bulk, the other according to the authorships of the hymns. According to the former the whole Samhitâ consists of 8 *ashtakas*; these, again, are divided into 64 *adhyâyas*; these into 2006 *vargas*; and the *vargas* into *richas*, the actual number of which is 10,417; and some say to have amounted to 10,616 or 10,622. According to the other method, the Samhitâ is divided into 10 *mandalas*; the *mandalas* into 85 *anuvâkas*, these into 1017 hymns, besides eleven spurious ones, called Vâlakhilyas, and 10,580 *richas*. The number of *padas*, or words, in this Samhitâ is stated as being 153,826, and that of the syllables is 432,000. The Nirukta mentions the Rig-veda in several places; and always with the designation of Dasatayyas, or the ten parts. And the same mode of designation is also found in the Prâtisâkhya-Sûtras. Another instance of the systematic arrangement of the *mandalas* is contained in the A'pri hymns; and there are only ten Á'pri-Súktas attached to the Rigveda. These Súktas consist properly of eleven verses, each of which is addressed to a separate deity; and they were evidently composed for sacrificial purposes. The chief object of the Á'pri hymns, and the motive which guided the priest to choose from among themselves according to the family to which his client belonged, are not so easy to explain. It is probable that the A'pri hymns were songs of reconciliation. Saunaka has given different names of metres in an Anukramaní. There are three Anukramanís to the Yajus. The Sáman has two different Anukramanís. For the Atharvan, there is only one Anukramaní, which is called the Brihatsarvánukramaní. The style of composition and the object of the different Anukramanís distinctly prove that they were framed at the close of the Vaidik age.

There is a class of works commonly designated Pariśishtas. They have Vaidik rituals and sacrifices for their subject matter. It is said that most of the Pariśishtas are the productions of Saunaka, &c. The Pariśishtas represent a distinct period of Indian literature, and they are evidently later than the Sútras. Such literary works as the Pariśishtas must be considered the last outskirts of Vaidik literature. But still they are Vaidik in character. The Parisishtas, on the whole, are indited in simple and felicitous diction. They were originally eighteen in number, but that number has now considerably exceeded. The Charanavyûha, though itself a Parisishta, supports this statement. There are a number of Parisishtas for each of the Vedas. For the Rig-veda there are only three; for the Sâma veda the number is only six; and according to the Charanavyûha there exist eighteen Parisishtas for the Yajur-veda. But Prof. Weber reckons them in round number seventy-four. The object of the Parisishtas is to supply the deficiencies in the Sûtras. They treat every thing in a popular and superficial manner. None of them were written probably before the middle of the third century, B. C. Though the Parisishtas are not held in the same estimation as other Vaidik works, yet they contain very interesting indications of the progress and decay of Hindu thought.

In former times the Vedas were the only source of knowledge and of truth to the Hindus. No one then ventured to carry on any controversy, or hold or spread any doctrine unwarranted by them, it being universally assumed that all doctrine must be based on, and all controversy must end in, what was taught by the Vedas. It was considered the height of atheism to speak one word against them. Thus it was that the supreme and unerring authority of the Vedas having been established, all theological controversy was at once nipped in the bud. On the other hand, the study of the Vedas became gradually extinct; the understanding and the explaining of their meanings became a hard task; the aims and objects of the *yajnas*, enjoined in them, were lost; and all religious works came to be encrusted with external ceremonies. In every country where religion becomes so dead and lifeless, religious changes begin to creep in. So did it fare with Indian society. First of all, Sákya, a man of uncommon wisdom and courage, the founder of Buddhism, opposed them, exposed the futility and the unreasonableness of such of their doctrines as the killing of animals, and proved the human authorship of the Vedas. Men were surprised at the first starting of these novel theories of Sákya. They had long ago relinquished the use of reason under the despotic government of the Vedas; but now again they entered the field of religious investigation, laid open by Sákya with renewed earnestness. But Sakya was not the first who opposed the selfish priesthood. Several centuries before him,

Visvámitra, of the royal caste, refused to submit to the hierarchical pretensions of the Brahmans, and succeeded in obtaining the privileges for which he determinately fought. King Janaka of Videha again followed him in the same track. The spread of Buddhism was simply owing to the fact that it aimed at a social reform, and more so to its pure and simple morality; rather than to the strength of its doctrinal points.

The doctrines of such a man as Sâkya naturally began to spread with the rapidity of fire borne by driving winds, and India became a spacious field for the waging of religious wars. Thus, within a short period, the Buddhists waxed very strong in this country; in the reign of Asoka, king of Magadha, the greater portion of it was converted to the religion of Sâkya. The Brahmans again roused themselves and determined upon putting down the victorious heretics. With this view they went into every part of the country, stirred up the dormant spirit of the Hindu kings, and fell to religious debates with the Buddhists. In this momentous religious warfare, Sankara A'chárya, who flourished in the 8th or 9th century,* played a most conspicuous and glorious part. He alone, as

* Colebrooke's Miscellaneous Essays, L p. 332.

a hermit, visited every part of India, defeated the Buddhists, one and all, with the sharpedged acuteness of his intellect, his extraordinary wisdom and knowlege of the Vedas, and finally carried the palm of universal conquest. Thus, being borne down in debate by the Brahmans, and persecuted by kings, the Buddhists left India to spread their religion in other countries.* But though the Buddhists were themselves expelled from the country, their doctrines did not all follow them out of it; on the contrary, these doctrines began, day by day, to strike deep root. And the doctrines of Sákya were a refuge even for Brahmans, who were unable to overcome the extreme difficulties of their own complicated system.† The transcendental doctrine of Nirvâna, or total annihilation, which Sâkya had proclaimed, was carefully picked up and nursed by the Hindu philosophers. Buddhism if examined by its own canonical works, cannot be freed from the charge of Nihilism. Sâkya himself not a Nihilist, was apparently an atheist. He does not gainsay either the existence of gods or that of God; but he denounces the former, and seems to be ignorant of the latter. If Nirvana was not complete annihi-

* Troyer's Râdjatarangini, ii. p. 390.
† Burnouf's History of Indian Buddhism, p. 196.

lation, it at any rate according to him, was absorption into a Divine essence. It was a relapse into that Being which is nothing but itself. The original meaning of Nirvana we can best know from the etymology of this technical term. Even a tyro in Sanskrit knows that Nirvāna means 'blowing out' and not absorption. The human soul when it reaches the acme of its full perfection, is blown out,[*] to use the phraseology of the Buddhists, like a lamp; it is not however absorbed, as the Brahmans express, like a drop in the ocean. We cannot at all events accept the term Nirvāna in the sense of an apotheosis of the human soul as it is taught in the Vedānta philosophy. It admits of question whether the term Nirvāna was coined by Sākya. Not merely different schools, but one and the same among the Buddhists appear to propound different theories as to the orthodox lexicography of this term.

The religion of the Vedas is an absurd system: Buddhism is equally absurd, but more philosophic. Buddhism was a revolt against the oppressive domination of the Brahmanic hierarchy. The devotion of the Buddhist ascetic was more disinterested. The Brahman idea of perfection was of an egotisti-

[*] Amara-kosha, s.v.

cal character. The meek spirit of Buddhism contrasts strongly with the haughtiness and arrogance of Brahmanism. We do not mean, however, to write the history of Buddhism; and we must therefore be satisfied with having given above a short account of the changes which occured just after the Vaidik period.

There is one more circumstance in connexion with the subject to which we wish to allude, before we close, and it has reference to the introduction of writing in ancient India. The greater portion of the vast ancient literature of India existed in oral tradition only, and was never reduced to writing. No man of any intelligence can easily imagine a civilized people unacquainted with the art of writing. If we are to understand that Hindu civilization could exist without a knowledge of writing, then it is needless to make reference to the arts, sciences, measures, and coins mentioned by Pâṇini in his Sûtras. From a certain rule of Pâṇini's Grammar (iv. 1. 49) we are convinced of the fact that he knew that writing was practised in countries beyond India. Pâṇini was a native of Sâlâtura or Gandhâra. Kâtyâyana and Patanjali define *yavanâni* as meaning 'the writing of the *Yavanas*.' The word *Yavana* occurs in Homer as Ἰάονες, which is no doubt connected with the Hebrew Yāvān. In later times it denotes especially the Arabs; but in earlier times it was exclusively applied to the Greeks as is evident from an example quoted in the commentary of Pāṇini's Grammar, 'yavanāḷḷ asyāna bhuñjate,' which alludes, no doubt, to Greek customs. Both Weber* and Müller† give a different meaning of the word *yavanānī*. M. Reinaud has given cogent reasons to prove that *yavanānī* means the writing of the Greeks. Benfey also understands by it 'Greek writing.' *Yavanānī* was generally used to signify *lipi*, or writing; which probably refers to the Greek character known in India by repute or perhaps actually used in the Panjab.

Müller says that in the Grammar of Pāṇini there is not a single word which shows that the Hindus knew the art of writing even when that learned work was composed. This assertion is a most novel and startling one, in as much as it is hard to conceive that a grammar, like that of Pāṇini, could be elaborated as it is now, without the advantage of written letters and signs in the days of the

---

* Indische Studien, I. p. 144; Ibid, iv. p. 89.
† History of Ancient Sanskrit Literature, p. 521.

author. Kâtyâyana and Patanjali not merely presuppose a knowledge of writing in Pâṇini, but affirm that the use he made of writing was one of the chief tools which assisted him in building up the technical structure of his work. Any person, that has ever looked into Pâṇini, must know that written accents were indispensable for his terminology. Pâṇini not unfrequently refers in his Sûtras to the grammarians who preceded him; which circumstance strengthens the argument in favor of the fact that writing was known even before Pâṇini's time. The word *lipikara* occurs in the Sûtras of Pâṇini; which can be adduced, in all fairness, to prove that the greatest Grammarian of India was acquainted with the art of writing. The root *likh* to write (*alekharachnyate*) in his Gaṇapâṭha is also conclusive on the point. He moreover teaches the formation of the word *lipikara* (iii. 2, 21). Paṭala, the name of a division in Sanskrit works, is a further proof that writing was known in ancient India.

The authors of the Sûtra works are found to apply the term paṭala to the short chapters of their works. Paṭala means covering, and a kind of creeping plant. It is, however, wholly absurd to suppose that chapters can be so called in a traditional work. It is only possible in a written one. Paṭala is almost synonymous with *liber* and βιβλος. "There is no word,' says Müller, 'for book, paper, ink, writing, &c., in any Sanskrit work of genuine antiquity."* This assertion of Müller clearly shows that he has overlooked some words which might have, on the contrary, removed all his doubts. He should have known that the object of the Vaidik hymns is not to tell us that the Aryans had reed and ink. It is most difficult to suppose that the human mind could ever be capable of composing in prose, volumes after volumes, on rituals, long series of commentaries, and elaborate works on theology, grammar, and lexicography, without any help of written letters. According to Wolf, prose composition is an evident and safe proof of a written literature as poetry without being committed to paper, could be easily composed and transmitted from one generation to another traditionally; but to compose any thing in prose is impossible without the help of writing; and still more impossible to transmit it from one generation to another and preserve it in its entirety traditionally.† There are undoubtedly records of astronomical observations which could not have been taken without the

* History of Ancient Sanskrit Literature, p. 512.
† Wolf's Prolegomena, lxi-lxxlii.

knowledge of numerical figures. We cannot help believing by the exact definition of words, which appear in Pâṇini, such as varṇa, kâra, kâṇḍa, patra, sûtra, adhyâya, grantha &c., that the use of written letters was not unknown or uncultivated in ancient India. The meaning of the word *grantha* is to string together, signifying the old method of stringing together a number of palm leaves, which constituted the chief material of books, just as in German a volume is called *Band*, from its being "bound." Prof. Weber holds that Pâṇini was perfectly acquainted with the art of writing; and the word *grantha*, which is frequently used by Pâṇini, alludes, according to its etymology, indisputably to written texts.* It answers etymologically to the Latin *textus*, as opposed to a traditional work. But Böhtlingk, and Roth say, on the contrary, that the word *grantha* refers merely to composition. Indeed, it may mean a literary composition. *Varṇa* applies merely to a written sign; and *kâra* to the uttered sound, and also to the written sign. *Akshara* means 'syllable;' and may sometimes therefore coincide in value with *kâra* and *varṇa*. *Akshara* signifying 'syllable' first occurs in the Samhitâ of the Yajus, and gives there the idea of writing. The word is

* Indische Studien, iv. p. 89.

also twice met with in the Ṛik; and there it signifies the measuring of speech (i. 164, 24 (47), and ix. 13, 3), and therefore may be used in the sense of 'syllable.' The Commentaries of Kâtyâyana, Patanjali and Kaiyata prove that Pâṇini's manner of defining an *adhikâra* (i. 3, 11), or heading rule, would have been impossible without writing. Here we will draw the attention of the reader to two words; and first to the word *ûrdhva*. It is used adverbially in the sense of 'after.'* It seems to us that the metaphorical sense of the word was first applied to passages in written books. And *ukṭya* is synonymous with *ûrdhva*. Pâṇini speaks of *repha*. Even Kâtyâyana arguing from its root, concludes that it is nothing else than *ra* itself; and the letter *repha* is found to be used in the Prâtiśâkhyas. The use of *repha* is also a proof that Pâṇini was not ignorant of writing. *Grantha* occurs four times in the texts of Pâṇini; and it is evident, beyond doubt, that *grantha* must mean a written or bound book. *Pustaka* is a Sanskrit word; and the derivation of the word may be traced to the root *pusta*. This root occurs in the Dhâtupâṭha. In ancient times barks and leaves of particular trees were used as writing materials for want of paper. The

* Manu, ix. 77.

Bhûrja-patra and the palm leaves were especially preferred. And to this day Bhûrja-patra and palm leaves are used for writing purposes. In Egypt this custom was also prevalent; and the very word paper is derived from 'papyrus' which means the bark of a reed.

The *Srauta-sûtras* of A'svalâyana, and the Prâtisâkhyas of the different Vedas afford numerous statements which cannot be explained without admitting a knowledge of letters in the authors of those ancient works. Since there is not one single allusion in the Vaidik hymns to any thing connected with writing, there are no such words as, writing, reading, paper, or pen in them. But this can never be a conclusive proof of the ignorance of the art of writing in ancient India. How were the gigantic works of ancient times divided into chapters and sections without any help of writing? How without a knowledge of numerals, were the cattle marked on their ears in order to identify them? Pânini has a *sûtra* (vi. 3, 115) in which he says that the owners of cattle were at his time in the habit of marking their beasts on the ears, with signs of a svastika, or magic figure of prosperity, a laddle, a pearl, &c.,' and also eight and five, which certainly, point to a knowledge of written letters or numerals at that period. Similarly the use of *lopa*, to express elision,* as opposed to the visibility of a letter points to language as existing in a written and not exclusively spoken form. It is impossible that an author could speak of a thing visible, literally or metaphorically, unless it were referable to his sense of sight. A letter which has undergone the effect of *lopa*, must, therefore, previously to its *lopa*, have been a visible or written letter to him. In the Grihya-Sûtras rules are given to be observed by Brahmans from the commencement of their existence to the last day of their life; but there does not appear a single word on the subject of their learning to write. There is, however, a sûtra 'patrai vedam pradâya vâchayet'; by which we must understand that here Veda means nothing else than Veda in the written form. Every one must now understand that Pânini was as proficient in writing as the cowherds of his time. It will not be rash to hold that the Vedas were preserved in writing at or before Pânini's time. And it could be shown that Pânini must have seen written Vaidik texts.† Now it is obvious that the ancient Hindus must have been acquainted with the art of writing. No question

---

* Pânini, i. 1,60 : अदर्शनं लोपः ।

† Pânini, vii. 1,76 : छन्दस्यपि दृश्यते ।

could be raised against the fact that the Hindus were acquainted with the art of writing before the time of Alexander; and the expressions of *likhita* and *likhāpita** occur in the inscriptions of Piyadasi, which are, no doubt, of the third century B. C. However, we shall not exceed a reasonable limit by assigning the 13th century B. C. for the origin of writing in India.

What was the alphabet that Pánini and his predecessors used, is a question that can hardly be answered positively since there are not sufficient data to decide it. But it was by no means Bactrian. The Bactrian is avowedly not full. Its vowels are few and at the same time not perfect, and even consonants deficient. In this state of the case the Bactrian could have been, by no means, originally adopted and used for a language most noted for its long and short vowels. To suppose that when a nation had once caught the idea of alphabetic writing, they would afterwards fail to devise a sufficient number of letters to meet their requirements, is quite absurd. From the circumstance that when the Aryans came to India, each part of the land was inhabited by the Dravidians who were considered to be autchthonous to the soil; and that in the natural course of events

* Manu, viii. 168.

the Aryans came in contact with those aborigines; the inference has been drawn that they must have got their alphabet from them and from no other source. But there is nothing to prove that those aborigines had a written literature at the time when the Aryans intruded on them and settled here. Not even now a single Dravidian book has been discovered, which may be considered to be of a pre-Vaidik era. The Dravidians were by no means a literary race, their ancient history is quite a blank; and the little that we know of them is from the writings of the Aryans themselves. That when the Dravidians themselves had no alphabet of their own, the Aryans are said to have borrowed one from them is so illogical that it scarcely calls for further notice. It is supposed by some that the Aryans did not originate an alphabet either before they migrated to India or after they settled there; they borrowed elsewhere. According to them the writing of the Aryans is of Semitic origin.* Were we to assume that they came to India before they had devised a system of alphabetic writing, it may not even be paradoxical to hazard an opinion more especially

* Benfey, Indien (in Ersch and Gruber's Encyclopaedia, 1840), p. 254; Weber's Indische Skizzen (1856), p. 127,ff.; and Burnell's Elements of South Indian Palaeography, p. 32.

when they are said to have left their primitive home in a far more advanced social state than their predecessors who had long before separated from them, and went forth in other directions, that such a highly intellectual race would originate it in their adopted country, without borrowing it from their neighbours.

APPENDIX.

The *PURUSHA SÚKTA*, or the 90th Hymn of the 10th Book of the Rig-veda Samhitá.

1. Purusha has a thousand heads, a thousand eyes, a thousand feet. On every side enveloping the earth, he overpassed (it) by a space of ten fingers. 2. Purusha himself is this whole (universe), whatever has been and whatever shall be. He is also the lord of immortality, since (or, when) by food he expands. 3. Such is his greatness, and Purusha is superior to this. All existences are a quarter of him; and three-fourths of him are that which is immortal in the sky. 4. With three quarters Purusha mounted upwards. A quarter of him was again produced here. He was then diffused everywhere over things which eat and things which do not eat. From him was born Viráj, and from Viráj, Purusha. When born, he extended beyond the earth, both behind and before. 6. When the gods performed a sacrifice with Purusha as the oblation, the spring was its butter, the summer its fuel, and the autumn its (accompanying) offering. 7. This victim, Purusha, born in the beginning, they immolated on the sacrificial grass. With him the gods, the Sádhyas, and the rishis sacrificed. 8. From that

universal sacrifice were provided curds and butter. It formed those aerial (creatures) and animals both wild and tame. 9. From that universal sacrifice sprang the rich and sáman verses, the metres, and the yajus. 10. From it sprang horses, and all animals with two rows of teeth; kine sprang from it; from it goats and sheep. 11. When (the gods) divided Purusha, into how many parts did they cut him up? what was his mouth? what arms (had he)? what (two objects) are said (to have been) his thighs and feet? 12. The Brahman was his mouth; the Rájanya was made his arms; the being (called) the Vaisya, he was his thighs; the Súdra sprang from his feet. 13. The moon sprang from his soul (menas), the sun from his eye, Indra and Agni from his mouth, and Váyu from his breath. 14. From his navel arose the air, from his head the sky, from his feet the earth, from his ear the (four) quarters: in this manner (the gods) formed the worlds. 15. When the gods, performing sacrifice, bound Purusha as a victim, there were seven sticks (stuck up) for it (around the fire), and thrice seven pieces of fuel were made. 16. With sacrifice the gods performed the sacrifice. These were the earliest ri   . These great powers have sought the sky, where   the former Sádhyas, gods.

John Muir.

Page 10, line 6.

When we read of any Rishi speaking of his own hymn as new, we must conclude that he was of course acquainted with many of the older hymns of the same kind. The relative antiquity of the different hymns can only be determined by their general contents, ideas, language, style, and metre. The old hymns however were displaced by the new; but the former were held as sacred as the latter. The authors of the new hymns had to borrow many thoughts and words from the old ones; and such repetitions often occur in their compositions. (*Langlois, Rig-veda, i. p. xiii*).

Page 13, line 7.

There are no traces to be met with in the hymns of the *Rig-veda* of the elaborate system of Yugas, Manvantaras, and Kalpas. But we frequently meet with the word *Yuga* which occurs in them in the sense of age, generation, or tribe (i. 139, 8; iii. 26, 3; vi. 8, 5; vi. 15, 8; vi. 36, 5; x. 94, 12).

Page 22, line 4 from the foot.

The Rishis sought from their gods every kind of temporal blessings, such as long life, food, riches, strength, offspring, cattle and rain. And they in like manner expected that those gods would direct their devotional acts, stimulate their poetical powers, and inspire them to compose hymns in honor of them. Hence we see the most distinct indications in some of the hymns of superhuman character ascribed to the Rishis themselves, and of divine influence which suggested their compositions.

Page 26, line 20.

The reference which is found in the Purusha-sûkta to the four different kinds of Vaidik compositions such as rich, sâman, chhandas, and yajus, distinctly proves the comparatively later date of the Sûkta. The Atharvan may be referred to under the appellation of chhandas (*Atharva-veda,* xi. 7, 24).

Page 14, line 16.

The Sâma-veda contains no extracts from any of the later hymns of the Rig-veda; and therefore it may be probable that the former had been compiled before the later portions of the latter were produced (*Weber's History of Indian Literature,* pp. 9, 62).

Page 15, line 12.

Burnell (Preface to the A´rsheya-Brâhmana, p. xvi ff.) and Aufrecht (Preface to the *Hymnen des*

Rig-veda, pp. xvi., xvii.) urge against the superior antiquity of the readings of the Sāyana, as compared with those of the Rik-Samhitā.

Page 21, line 12.

In the Atharva-veda the Bahlikas are mentioned (v. 22, 5, 7, 14); while the *Rig-veda* is quite ignorant of such people. At any rate the oldest Indians must have been acquainted with them. There is nothing of poetical conception in the Atharvan. It is rather full of sorcery and of priestly vagaries and pretensions. In it there is also every mark of a complete development of ritual. It contains no hymn addressed to Vishnu, nor is there any hymn addressed to Indra such as we find in the *Rik-Samhitā*. But there is a hymn dedicated to Varuna which is remarkable in every respect. This hymn formed an oath to be taken by a witness (x. 5, 36, 44; xvi. 7, 8; xvi. 8, 1). Though there are in the Atharvan indications of a full-blown polytheism, yet there are some traces to be found of a progress towards monotheism.

Page 44, line 16.

The *Rig*- and the Atharva-vedas throw much light on the mutual relations of the different classes of Indian society at the time when they were composed. From the later hymns of the Rig-veda we learn that the priesthood had already become a profession; but there are other indications also which justify the conclusion that there was no discrimination of profession; and even there are numerous references to be found in all parts of the hymn-collection to a variety of ranks, classes, and professions however without any rigid prescriptions about them. The three highest castes stood in a more intimate relation with each other either in point of descent or culture, than any of them did to the fourth.

Page 44, line 11.

The term Vaisya does not occur in any other hymns of the Rig-veda, but in the Purusha-sûkta; and only once in the Atharvan (v. 17, 9). The Vaisyas formed the mass of the people; it being derived from the word *vis* which means the general community.

Page 52, line 17, note.

The slaughter of a cow on the arrival of a distinguished guest was invariably practised in India. This custom was so widely prevalent that *goghna* or "cow-killer" came to pass as a term for such a guest. Even Pāṇini has given the etymology of

(185)

"cow-killer" in the sense of a guest (iii. 4, 73 ; गावीनी संवाने.|) But it appears that the cow and one of its products (gomūtra) came to be regarded as sacred in the days of Patanjali, whose date has been fixed in the middle of the 2nd century B. C.

Page 66, line 1 from the foot.

Max Müller, in his Chips from a German Workshop, i. 33, says that "The religion of the Veda knows of no idols. The worship of idols in India is a secondary formation, a later degradation of the more primitive worship of ideal gods." But on the other hand, Dr. Bollensen, in the Journal of the German Oriental Society, xxii. 587ff., contends against this opinion. If we are to take into consideration that our ancestors were of a deep poetical temperament and a delicate imaginative power, it becomes highly probable that the gods would receive a variety of ideal or human forms and epithets; and they would be invoked to discharge the functions which the poetical feeling of their worshippers alone has attributed to them. So when we read of such epithets as *nripeças* (R. V. iii. 4,5), &c., and of expressions as *rûpa, vapus,* and *sandris,* we are to understand them as used in a metaphorical sense.

Page 78, line 29.

Parjanya is the thundering rain-god. He appears to have been associated with Váta and Agni; but was decidedly distinct from Indra. He is called the son of Dyaus, and the father of the soma plant. He is represented as the lord of all moving creatures. He presides over the lightning, the thunder, the rain; and is said to impregnate the plants.

Brahmanaspati or Brihaspati is described as the offspring of the two Worlds. He appears sometimes to be identical with Indra; but is elsewhere distinguished from Agni. He is styled the father of the gods, and is possessed of all divine attributes. He is bright, pure, clear-voiced, opulent, and a remover of disease. He is called a priest, and intercedes with the gods on behalf of men. He is the protector of the pious; and saves them from all dangers.

Trita A'ptya, Ahirbudhnya, and Aja Ekapád are minor divinities. Trita is conjoined with the Maruts, Váta or Váyu, and Indra. He is called A'ptya; and his abode is hidden. He bestows long life. Ahirbudhnya is the Dragon of the deep, and resides in the atmospheric ocean. Aja Ekapád is probably a storm-god.

Page 112, line 4, note.

On the subject of the priority of the hymns to the

Brâhmanas the commentator of the Taittirîya, or Black Yajur-veda, Samhitâ thus delivers himself:—" Although the Veda is formed both of Mantra and Brâhmana, yet as the Brâhmana consists of an explanation of the Mantras, it is the latter which were at first recorded." (p. 9 of the Calcutta edition).

Page 140, *line* 11.

The Mantras, the Brâhmanas, the A'ranyakas, and the Upanishads are designated under the term of Sruti; while the term Smriti includes the Vedângas, the Sûtras, Srauta and Grihya, &c. Sruti means revelation; and Smriti recollection. The Mantras are either metrical hymns or prose forms of prayer, in which the praises of the gods are celebrated, and their blessing is invoked. The Rik and the Sâman consist of hymns of the former description. The Brâhmanas arose out of the hymns, and so stand next to them. They embrace liturgical regulations regarding the ceremonial employment of the hymns, and the celebration of the various rites of sacrifice; and also include such treatises as the A'ranyakas and the Upanishads. The A'ranyakas and the Upanishads are theological treatises, and bear the same character as some of the older portions of the Brâhmanas.

They give very distinct indications of spiritual aspirations, and also of ideas of a speculative and mystical character such as we find in the hymns, and in the earlier portions of the Brâhmaṇas; but only with this exception that in those treatises they have been further matured as they developed in the minds of subsequent generations of the sages.

Page 122, line 2.

The legend of a Flood, according to M. Burnouf, is not in its origin Indian, but was most probably derived from a Semitic source, whether Hebrew or Assyrian (*Bhâgavata-Purâna, iii. Préf. pp. li., lii.-liv*). But Professor Weber from the legend of Manu in the Satapatha-Brâhmaṇa, which he for the first time brought to light, has proved that the tradition was really current in India at a much earlier period than Burnouf thought; and it was not imported into that country from any of the Semitic sources (*Indische Studien, i. p. 160 ff*).

Page 154, line 3.

From a comparison of the Brâhmaṇas with the Kalpa books it appears that the difference between them is most indispensable. They are found to treat in the most elaborate manner of the entire system of divine worship, though in quite a different sense in both of them. The Kalpa books establish the whole course of the rites of worship, direct which of the priests has to take part at each of the stages of the sacred rites, what hymns are to be recited, and further define the time and the place for the celebration of those rites. But the object of a Brâhmana is very different from the Kalpa works; its subject being the 'brahma,' the sacred element in the rite; from which we are to draw the most valuable information regarding the early conceptions on divine things (*Roth's Introduction to the Nirukta, p. xxiv ff*).

www.ingramcontent.com/pod-product-compliance
Lightning Source LLC
Chambersburg PA
CBHW020933230426
43666CB00008B/1663